Mark Cazalet, George and the Dragon, Manchester Cathedral.
Photo by Tony Hardy

Redcrosse

Praise for
Redcrosse

'How do we think about identity in ways that don't reflect anxiety, fear of the other, uncritical adulation of our past and all the other pitfalls that surround this subject? The *Redcrosse* project manages to negotiate these difficulties with immense imaginative energy and honesty: no sour notes, no attempt to overcompensate by desperately over-apologetic rhetoric, simply a recovery of deep roots and generous vision. As much as it takes its cue from Spenser, it's a contemporary working out of some of the great and inexhaustible legacy of Blake, a unique contribution to what is often a pretty sterile discussion of who we are in these islands.'

DR ROWAN WILLIAMS, *Archbishop of Canterbury, UK*

'This is a valuable and generous book. Valuable because it exemplifies how profound and ancient symbols of our culture may become active again in the modern imagination. Generous because this project yearns to give and include, to listen and confess, undaunted by the authority of the past or by the face of opposition.'

LIAM SEMLER, *University of Sydney, Australia, and President of the Australasian Universities Language and Literature Association*

'A moving and provocative book, often baffling, and even knowingly quixotic in its accounts of the hard work of these devoted poets, scholars, clerics, and theologians in shaping from Spenser's wild allegorical romance a "questing liturgy" for the English Church of today.

It is far from what the ordinary reader of Spenser (if such a creature exists!) might expect, but the questions this book poses stay with me.'

KENNETH GROSS, *University of Rochester, USA, and author of* Spenserian Poetics: Idolatry, Iconoclasm, and Magic; Shylock is Shakespeare; *and most recently* Puppet: An Essay on Uncanny Life

'A collective quest for renewal and reform, which invests in the future of poetry by re-wedding liturgy and literature. Assembling a stellar team of poets, scholars, and clergy, this civic experiment with the legacy of Spenser and the legend of St. George aims to reconnect people and peoples, faith and faiths, through the participatory power of the poetic Word.'

JULIA REINHARD LUPTON, *University of California, Irvine, USA, and author of* Thinking with Shakespeare *and* Citizen-Saints

'The *Redcrosse* project has demonstrated how true liturgy is a quest for liturgy and a continuing self-questioning. It cannot evade the specificity of place and circumstance, even though these might lean towards bias: being reconciled to the tendril of our own path is our only way to attain a specific glimpse of the universal. So here the ambivalent legacy of the English Red Cross and the cult of St George are embraced and yet ritually purged with the help of the mythopoeic vision of Edmund Spenser: the blood of ugly victory becomes the pelican blood of suffering and searching, and triumph is itself turned into the miraculous arrival of always particular and always social grace. The essays in the volume take forward the task of the liturgy and open the way to more such awakenings in future.'

CATHERINE PICKSTOCK, *Emmanuel College, Cambridge, UK, and author of* After Writing: On the Liturgical Consummation of Philosophy

Redcrosse

Remaking Religious Poetry for Today's World

Edited by
Ewan Fernie

BLOOMSBURY
LONDON • BERLIN • NEW YORK • SYDNEY

Bloomsbury Academic
An imprint of Bloomsbury Publishing Plc

50 Bedford Square	175 Fifth Avenue
London	New York
WC1B 3DP	NY 10010
UK	USA

www.bloomsbury.com

First published 2013

© Ewan Fernie and Contributors, 2013

All rights reserved. No part of this publication may be reproduced or transmitted in any form or by any means, electronic or mechanical, including photocopying, recording, or any information storage or retrieval system, without prior permission in writing from the publishers.

Ewan Fernie has asserted his right under the Copyright, Designs and Patents Act, 1988, to be identified as Author of this work.

No responsibility for loss caused to any individual or organization acting on or refraining from action as a result of the material in this publication can be accepted by Bloomsbury Academic or the author.

British Library Cataloguing-in-Publication Data
A catalogue record for this book is available from the British Library.

ISBN: HB: 978-1-4411-7858-9
PB: 978-1-4411-3899-6

Library of Congress Cataloging-in-Publication Data
Redcrosse : remaking religious poetry for today's world / edited by Ewan Fernie.
p. cm.
Includes bibliographical references and index.
ISBN 978-1-4411-7858-9 (hardcover)– ISBN 978-1-4411-3899-6 (pbk.)– ISBN 978-1-4411-5730-0 (pdf)– ISBN 978-1-4411-5691-4 (epub) 1. Religious poetry--Authorship. 2. National characteristics, English, in literature. 3. Religion and poetry. I. Fernie, Ewan, 1971-

PR508.R4R43 2012
821.009'382–dc23

2012011974

Typeset by Fakenham Prepress Solutions, Fakenham, Norfolk NR21 8NN
Printed and bound in India

For Andrew Taylor, who did so much to make it happen;
And – why not? – for St George.

Photograph credit: Tony Hardy

Contents

Contributors xiii
Acknowledgements xvii

Part One Reflections 1

1 Through the Red Cross, *Ewan Fernie* 3

2 For Real, *Salley Vickers* 45

3 A Desire for the Impossible, *Andrew Shanks* 57

4 The Poet's Tale, *Michael Symmons Roberts* 93

5 Fight the Good Fight?, *Sarah Apetrei* 105

6 From Romance to Ritual: *Redcrosse* and Spenser's *Faerie Queene*, *John Milbank* 133

Part Two Redcrosse 179

Redcrosse: A New Celebration of England and St George by Ewan Fernie, Michael Symmons Roberts, Jo Shapcott and Andrew Shanks, and featuring a new poem from Andrew Motion and the Collect for St George's Day 181

Index 201

Contributors

Sarah Apetrei is Departmental Lecturer in Ecclesiastical History at the University of Oxford and Acting Director of Studies in Theology at Keble College. She is author of *Women, Feminism and Religion in Early Enlightenment England* and co-editor of forthcoming books on *Women and Religion in Britain, 1660–1760* and *Jacob Boehme: An Introduction to His Thought and Its Reception over Four Centuries*. Attracted to misfits and dissenting voices, and to those who have imagined heaven on earth in the most startling forms, she is currently writing a book about the mystics and prophets who sought to transcend confessional politics in an early modern Europe that was ravaged by religious wars. This will make the surprising claim that mystical theology made an important contribution to the British Enlightenment.

Ewan Fernie is Professor of Shakespeare Studies at the Shakespeare Institute, University of Birmingham. He was Principal Investigator of '*The Faerie Queene* Now: Remaking Religious Poetry for Today's World', and leader of the *Redcrosse* project. He is the author of *Shame in Shakespeare*, editor of *Spiritual Shakespeares* and co-ordinating editor of *Reconceiving the Renaissance*. His latest work is *The Demonic: Literature and Experience* (Routledge). He has recently completed a *Macbeth* novel with Simon Palfrey, with whom he is also General

Editor of the 'Shakespeare Now!' series of short, provocative books published by Continuum. He writes a blog called *Shakespearience* for the Shakespeare Birthplace Trust.

John Milbank is Professor in Religion, Politics and Ethics at the University of Nottingham. He is the author of several books, of which the most well-known is *Theology and Social Theory* and the most recent *Being Reconciled: Ontology and Pardon*. He is one of the editors of the *Radical Orthodoxy* collection of essays which occasioned much debate. In general he has endeavoured in his work to resist the idea that secular norms of understanding should set the agenda for theology and has tried to promote the sense that Christianity offers a rich and viable account of the whole of reality. At the same time he tends to insist that Christianity is itself eclectic. He has sustained interests in developing a left-leaning political and social theology, and his current work, on the gift and the Trinity, brings together all of these concerns.

Andrew Motion was Poet Laureate from 1999 until 2009. His work has received the Arvon/Observer Prize, the John Llewelyn Rhys Prize, the De Moffart Art Prize and the Dylan Thomas Prize. In 1994 his biography of Philip Larkin was awarded the Whitbread Prize for Biography, and shortlisted for the NCR Award. *The Lamberts* won the Somerset Maugham Award. He was knighted for his services to literature in 2009. He is Professor of Creative Writing at Royal Holloway, University of London. His new collection of poems is *The Cinder Path* (Faber) and *Ways of Life: Places, Painters and Poets* (Faber) is his latest collection of essays.

Andrew Shanks is Canon Theologian at Manchester Cathedral, and co-ordinated Manchester Cathedral's participation in the *Redcrosse* project. He has previously zig-zagged between academic and full-time ecclesiastical work, and is the author of many books, including – most relevantly in the present context – *'What Is Truth?' Towards a Theological Poetics*. His latest book is *Hegel and Religious Faith: Divided Brain, Atoning Spirit*. Manchester Cathedral has for some years played host to an International Religious Poetry Competition; it has appointed a poet in residence; and is in general keen to be a place of experimentation with regard to the interplay between poetry and liturgy.

Jo Shapcott won the Queen's Gold Medal for Poetry in 2011, when she also won the Costa Prize for her collection *Of Mutability*. *Her Book: Poems 1988–1998* consists of a selection of poetry from three earlier collections: *Electroplating the Baby*, which won the Commonwealth Poetry Prize, *Phrase Book*, and *My Life Asleep*, which won the Forward Poetry Prize. She has won the National Poetry Competition twice. She has a Cholmondeley Award and is a Fellow of the Royal Society of Literature. She is Professor of Poetry at Royal Holloway, University of London, and President of the Poetry Society.

Michael Symmons Roberts is a poet, novelist, and Professor of Poetry at Manchester Metropolitan University. He has won the Whitbread Poetry Award, and been shortlisted for the Griffin International Poetry Prize, the Forward Prize, and twice for the T. S. Eliot Prize. He has also received major awards from the Arts Council and the Society of Authors. His latest collection of poetry is *The Half Healed*. His continuing collaboration with composer James MacMillan has led to two BBC Proms choral commissions, song cycles, music theatre works and an opera for the Welsh National Opera – *The Sacrifice* – which won the RPS Award for opera.

Salley Vickers is an English novelist, who also writes poetry and has been an academic teacher of English and a Jungian psychotherapist.

She is a consultant to the Liturgical Commission of the Church of England and regularly lectures on the connections between literature and religion and literature and psychology. Poetry and religion also recur in her novels, which include the word-of-mouth bestseller *Miss Garnet's Angel, Mr Golightly's Holiday, The Other Side of You, Dancing Backwards* and *Where Three Roads Meet*, a retelling of the Oedipus myth to Sigmund Freud in the last months of his life.

Acoustic Triangle and Royal Holloway Choir during Redcrosse *at St George's Chapel, Windsor.* Copyright Doug Harding

Acknowledgements

Ewan Fernie, Michael Symmons Roberts, Jo Shapcott and Andrew Shanks wrote *Redcrosse: A New Celebration of England and St George*.

With help from, in Windsor, Sarah Apetrei, David Fuller, Graham Holderness, Monawar Hussain, Kevin Morris, Ben Quash, David Ruiter, Andrew Taylor and Salley Vickers; and, in Manchester, Pam Elliott, Rachel Mann, Jan Dean, Michael Powell and Albert Radcliffe.

It features a new, opening poem by Andrew Motion.

It was premiered on Thursday 17 March at 7.00 p.m. in St George's Chapel, Windsor and on Sunday 8 May 2011 at 5.30 p.m. in Manchester Cathedral.

Tim Garland wrote the music.

Acoustic Triangle – Tim Garland, Malcolm Creese and Gwilym Simcock – played it.

The Choir of Royal Holloway College, University of London, sang it.

Redcrosse was co-ordinated by Ewan Fernie and Andrew Shanks, and is one outcome of 'The Faerie Queene Now' project. Ewan Fernie initiated this overall project with Simon Palfrey, encouraged by their previous conversations and shared projects. Andrew Taylor administered it, and did much more than required. This book is dedicated to him, and St George.

Elisabeth Dutton helped with the staging. She and her ensemble performed it in Windsor.

The Windsor event was part of the Windsor Spring Festival. An additional feature of the Manchester event was the presence of the George and Dragon processional 'giants', made by a team from the Booth Centre for the Homeless, under the artistic guidance of Paul Devereaux. David Fuller stepped in to 'be' Andrew Motion at Windsor, when Andrew was unable to be there. Doug Harding took the fabulous photos in Windsor which are reprinted by kind permission of the Dean and Canons of Windsor, and Tony Hardy took the impressive shots of the Manchester event, of which Liam Hardy made some great video. Mark Cazalet allowed us to make his inspiring painting of George and the dragon our frontispiece, and to reproduce the reredos painting of which it is part in Andrew Shanks' chapter below.

We are grateful for financial support from: Arts and Humanities Research Council (AHRC); Economic and Social Research Council (ESRC); Religion and Society; London Centre for Arts and Cultural Exchange (LCACE); Arts Council of England; PRS Foundation for Music; Royal Holloway, University of London; English Department, Royal Holloway; University of Birmingham. The making of the Manchester 'giants' was funded by Awards for All and the Church Urban Fund.

Further thanks to: Linda Woodhead and Rebecca Catto, John Milbank, Rebecca Warren Heys, Gilly Myers, Anne Varty, Marta Baker, Theodora Papadopoulou, Deanna, Rab and Heather Fernie, Shan and Charlie Turner, Eric S. Mallin, Jeremy and Irene Newton,

Acknowledgements

Elleke Boehme, Kiernan Ryan, Christie Carson, Stephen Regan, Jonathan Dollimore, Paul Edmondson, Stanley Wells, Kate McLuskie, Michael Dobson, Paul Hamilton, Mohamed Salim Said, Philippa Kelly, Liam Semler and AULLA, Geraldine Collinge and the RSC, Jane Woodward and Coventry Cathedral, Alastair Niven and his team at Cumberland Lodge, Martin Denny and the Windsor Festival, Farah Karim Cooper and Shakespeare's Globe, Gary McKeone and St George's House, Graham Henderson and Poet in the City, the anonymous readers at Bloomsbury books, and the supportive and acute Commissioning Editor, David Avital.

We are very grateful to all who have helped!

Part One

Reflections

Redcrosse *at Manchester Cathedral.* By Tony Hardy

1
Through the Red Cross

Ewan Fernie

'What is this England?' asks the minister at the start of the *Redcrosse* liturgy which is printed at the end of this book. 'We have a patron saint, but what does he stand for? We have a flag.'

Yes, but most of us take it for granted, or are even faintly embarrassed by it.

And yet, this stark symbol of a blood-red cross on a white background purports to represent us, as a people, as a nation, and often it actually does, in this country and round the world. Shouldn't we, then, turn our urgent attention to it? Shouldn't we inspect and interpret it – turning it over and over in imagination, as Andrew Shanks does in his psalm in the *Redcrosse* liturgy – with the utmost commitment and rigour, energetically repudiating all the mean, unworthy things for which it has been recruited and waved, while at the same time exploring and imagining for it better, indeed the best possible, most ambitious meanings?

And those meanings, insofar as they exceed narrow self-interest, will be moral; insofar as they exceed any particular or limited interest *at all*, religious.

The red cross seems to offer the English solidarity, but can such solidarity avoid the hostility to others it has so often entailed? What is an English world-view, and what should it be? What would it mean to look at the world afresh – as if for the first time – *through* the red cross? Would it just be to squint through a visor? That would be very depressing. And what if you couldn't get the Helmet of Hostility off? Could it, quite differently, be to look through a wound? And could it, just possibly, be *both*, so that the quest and struggle for an ideal Englishness becomes premised on a vulnerable openness? That seems more promising. And the liturgical text we wrote for St George's Day ends with the revelation and remaking of a ROSY cross in the hope that just such a struggle for openness might enable a new flourishing.

But I'm getting ahead of myself and I need to take you back in time for, whimsical though it may be, *Redcrosse* actually happened, and not once but twice; and it's due to happen again, we hope many times. Perhaps you will want to make it happen yourself, using the liturgical text at the back of this book. But let's return, for a moment, to 2011…..

The first time we're in St George's Chapel, Windsor, under the auspices of the Windsor Spring Festival. It is of course a perfect place for a new celebration of England and St George, almost an unrivalled one, with prime royal associations; the home of the Order of the Garter. But the fact there are armed guards outside is a reminder that this heritage is valuable but potentially embattled, a questionable, even a hated thing for some. And this is sharpened by the irony that it's not actually St George's but St Patrick's Day! (St George has, in 2011, had to be moved to make way for Easter Saturday.) Patrick seems to accuse us because Edmund Spenser, author of that English epic, *The Faerie Queene*, in many ways the well-spring of inspiration for *Redcrosse*, was a brutal colonialist in Ireland. Tainted well, then.

And it's difficult to resist the thought that here in Windsor on this day power conflicts with spirit.

But we're actually disposed to see that as rather a good thing. Because what we've prepared is a new poetic liturgy for real and guilty people. Not for 'beautiful souls' who want to stand perfectly aloof from the world; nor for wishful patriots who wish to side-step the fact of our country's fallenness. Ours is a civic liturgy that seeks to affirm and celebrate England and St George but only in their renovation, in confession and absolution, in rededication to the struggle and the quest.

Everyone's settling in the nave now, and each of us has been given a red rose.

God, it's a beautiful place! With its soaring, spreading, fan-vaulted ceiling in lightly honeyed stone. So much head-space. So much space to transcend in! No excuse for remaining shut up in ourselves.

There's an atmosphere of undetermined expectancy. Nobody knows quite what's going to happen, not even those of us who devised the event and wrote the text! Because it's something of a new thing this, neither an arts event, nor a religious service, but somehow both. And so much depends on audience or congregational participation.

What is lost in familiarity we hope will be gained in freshness. And perhaps that freshness will refresh our sense of the old familiar rituals, of how they work and what they're for.

We'd like *Redcrosse* to stimulate a new sense of the civic and religious possibilities for our own time.

Just so long as it doesn't fail; just so long as it carries these people with it; just so long as none of them *giggles*.

*

'What is this England?

What is this country called to be, and to become?'

So says the celebrant, before remarking we are so many different people, and praying we might be opened up to one another's otherness.

He then conjures for our collective imaginations, with the help of a new poem from Andrew Motion, the figure of a new St George – a younger George, always changed and changing in the quest, 'the symbol of our restlessness'. We are asked to accept him as our champion, and we do.

It is in the spirit of this new St George that we go on our symbolic journey, looking for meaning and value – looking, indeed, for God – in the elemental heart of life. As we return to our places in the nave we surrender our roses, which the celebrant asks us to see as symbolic of our prayers for ourselves and us all. From these roses a new flag is made. Choral music has played throughout, but now it really goes to town, elaborating and decorating the themes of the service.

'Make manifest the openness that will unite us all at last.'

When the Choir jubilantly sings 'Unite!', the flag is raised as a flag of prayers which together compose one great prayer of solidarity, as it has been enacted and, we hope, achieved, at least for the duration of this service.

No-one giggled.

*

The second time we're in the much darker interior of Manchester Cathedral, but the occasion is more folksy, festive and joyous. Again there are about a hundred and fifty people in the congregation. And this time they are truly different sorts: from a fair few in dog collars, to the homeless people who made the Catalan giants which are a special feature of the Manchester event. These giants stand approximately fifteen foot proud. A black George with wire-clippers in an England football shirt, a touch of gentle inspiration on his face. A disconsolate dragon whom this George is surely about to liberate. They more than anything else have roused the ire of the British National Party.

There are protests on Nick Griffin's website; a National Front website (www.national-front.org.uk/blackgeorge.htm, since disappeared) has called for a counter demonstration; a torrent of perhaps more than a hundred pieces of hatemail have been received (we didn't keep them all). But, to our relief, no protestors actually show up.

And our black George is so fine, I'd like to think – the very formula for wishful thinking! – he would quietly have outfaced all violence.

In Manchester, we move around more, from station to station: through the waving foliage of a wandering wood; through voluble air that speaks a psalm of many voices, and into the dragon's mouth for the fire sermon, before being laved in water song and sprinkled from the font. There is a shambling oneness to our motion which is liberally permitting and strangely beautiful. And now and again, through the masonry and the tracery of carving, George and the dragon gently loom. It's a bit like being in a surrealist painting! The flag of solidarity is made afresh.

As if to show that each time it must be.

For unity, solidarity, is a work in progress.

There is a great and palpable happiness when the service ends. And yes, maybe one or two giggles, but they are giggles of delight.

*

Such is the story to date of *Redcrosse: A New Celebration of England and St George*. Its premiere in St George's Chapel, Windsor Castle, took place in March 2011, and it happened in Manchester Cathedral in May of the same year; we hope it will be taken up for St George's Days now George has got his day back. Meanwhile it has been adopted by the Royal Shakespeare Company for Coventry Cathedral's fiftieth jubilee celebrations in autumn 2012; indeed, if everything goes to plan, the book you now hold in your hand will have been launched on the occasion of that service.

I directed the project and wrote *Redcrosse* with the creative theologian Andrew Shanks and three major contemporary English poets: Andrew Motion, Michael Symmons Roberts and Jo Shapcott. We also worked with two local groups of consultants in Windsor and Manchester, which brought together scholars, artists and theologians from different faith traditions, including Islam. Since we wanted to make something representative, we felt we should consult plenty of people! All of them made a major contribution to *Redcrosse*, and they and others who helped are named in the acknowledgements above.

We commissioned new music from the jazz/classical composer Tim Garland, for the Acoustic Triangle trio and Royal Holloway College Choir; the wonderful music Garland delivered mobilised many traditional motifs and themes in a spirit of improvising openness which seemed to make of all the past a work in progress, which was just what we were aiming at in our text. In Manchester, we commissioned the Catalan-style giant puppets from the Booth Centre for the Homeless under the artistic direction of Paul Devereaux.

Redcrosse seems to have met a need of the moment and it has won considerable funding: from the Arts and Humanities Research Council/Economic and Social Research Council 'Religion and Society' programme (a sizeable initial grant, this one); from the Arts Council of England; from the PRS for Music Foundation; from the London Centre for Arts and Cultral Exchange; from Awards for All and the Church Urban Fund. The RSC, Birmingham University and the Cathedral raised the money to put on the Coventry *Redcrosse*. But, importantly, *Redcrosse* could be done without any money.

It takes its title from and was particularly inspired by Spenser's first book of *The Faerie Queene*, *The Legend of the Knight of the Red Crosse, or of Holinesse*. This itself offers a new vision of the symbol of the red cross and the story of St George. Spenser offered positive inspiration, but also (as already hinted) usefully presented us with some of the problems, involved in our own later attempt to retell the archaic and sometimes xenophobic story of The Red Crosse Knight, and indeed of the Englishness he stands for, in and for the present.

Redcrosse is, very expressly, an attempt to intervene in – to refurbish, to *reimagine* – the story of Englishness the English tell themselves. But no, I should say, the story of Englishness *we English* tell *ourselves*; for that shift into the first person plural is indicative of a move in this project from more familiar scholarly procedures of more detached cultural critique to cultural *participation*.

Redcrosse started as an academic project and 'we murder to dissect', as Wordsworth puts it in his poem 'The Tables Turned', but criticism needn't be an exclusively analytical vocation, always following creativity. The position of the scholar in regard to our foundational stories need not be either wistfully nostalgic or critically superior, nor some curious mixture of the two; it can instead be one of renovating involvement. Literary scholarship can be creative, storytelling infused with critical energy.

This question of participation in wider social life is now a main and controversial criterion of academic funding bodies and research assessment in the UK under the banner of 'impact', and as such it is often – often rightly – resented. But the question of what effect academic work will have on the life of our society is a real and sensible one. It is certainly one that the pre-eminent literary critic of our time, Stephen Greenblatt, worries over in the nearest thing he has written to a theoretical manifesto, the co-authored *Practising New Historicism*. In that book, he offers the figure of the 'wicked son', who participates in Jewish ritual, albeit in a negative or critical fashion, as a model for the engaged academic.[1] This confrontation with the big question of what kind of contribution scholarship makes to human life is something for which Greenblatt is surely to be lauded. Such are the pressures of the contemporary academy that many scholars don't have the time or energy to look beyond the purview of the refereed journal and their particular specialism. But if in a larger, super-personal view the negative energy of the critic can serve the betterment of the general conversation and the social practices it engenders, as Greenblatt suggests, I want to suggest there are reasons to believe that literary scholarship may be on the cusp of a new opportunity to make a more positive contribution to contemporary civic life.

The biggest change in the internal structure in English Departments in recent memory is the widespread introduction of creative writers and writing. Sooner or later this is bound to have a profound effect on the discipline of literary studies. Creativity and criticism may operate in closer partnership than they have at any time in English-language culture, with critical form and practice becoming more and more creative, and criticism operating with and even inside a positive creative act, contributing more affirmatively to social reproduction and transformation. And if criticism and creativity are to come together in this mutually intensifying way, I for one can think of no better task for them to work on than the critical reinvention of the foundational stories we inherit.

The effort documented in this book, which brought together poets, critics and theologians to create a new poetic liturgy partly inspired by Spenser, is very much an attempt to rise to that challenge.

A word about the style the book is written in. Given our effort to bring scholarship in conjunction with poetry and religion into the wider world of national life, it would be wrong to reflect on what we did in standard, 'academics-only' discourse. Instead, we *tell the story*, from various angles, of our collaborative creation of and participation in a new poetic liturgy for St George's Day, as well as publishing the full text of that liturgy for the first time (though it's been quoted on radio and in various local and national papers). It's appropriate to present the project in something resembling narrative form because, unlike most academic initiatives, it came to fruition in a repeatable, nationally significant *event*. Our liturgy itself attempts to tell a new, hopeful and involving story about what our country is and could be; and, severally and together, our reflections on it attempt the same thing – although, admittedly, all sorts of things foreign to your average story, including literary criticism, theology, spiritual autobiography, cultural history and political commentary, including church politics, are part of this one! Still, this is not a book that could without utterly betraying its subject simply fall back on the special procedures, even the special pleading, of academic style. It is written by academics and non-academics who came together in what we hope isn't an entirely quixotic attempt to address the nation as such.

This is not at all to say that we wish to disown the academic origins of the project. Nor that *every* essay that follows fights shy of scholarly gravity and expertise. Some things can't be put simply, though the liturgy at the end of the book does, perforce, try to communicate with everybody who might participate in it. Our project was initiated by a generous academic grant – it is unwise as well as ungracious to bite the hand that feeds you – and it was sustained throughout by all the combined expertise that we and our advisors could muster in English literature and theology as well as other fields. I have said that our work entailed a movement from detached cultural critique to participation, but that participation very much involved critique. Indeed, I hope it will be everywhere apparent that our creative work was in fact inspired by and involved a *maximally critical* critique of cheap, resentful or retrograde notions of nation and religion.

Having said that, and while the academy is central to critical culture in this country, it is important to remember criticism doesn't *belong* to the academy; it's too important for that! And to the extent that it does seem to, it surely needs to be brought back into conjunction with more immediate concerns of personal, political, national, international and religious life. This, partly, for the sake of criticism: because if it is to be properly critical, surely criticism needs to be *self*-critical? As it cannot be if it remains sealed off in its professionalized position in the Universities. More than this, any self-referring and self-enclosed scholasticism sees less, and sees what it does see less well, than more engaged kinds of thinking. And then, personal, institutional and creative life have so much to gain from an infusion of criticism! A more critical creative culture is just likely to be a better one: more ambitious, more refined and more truthful.

It is also true that our creative fusion of criticism and creativity in an effort to refashion the story of St George and Englishness inevitably involves a certain departure from and challenge to current academic practice beyond matters of style. I am myself, I do not blush to admit it, a Professor of English. And in certain central respects, *Redcrosse* contradicts, or at least exists in significant tension with, the story my discipline most habitually tells at this stage of its historical development: that it is critical, pluralist, globalised, secular (at least in the sense of standing aloof from any particular religious position). In the wake of decades of powerful poststructuralist and postcolonial critique – of power, authority, imperialism – the scope for positive present-day English patriotism, and certainly for a positive English *religion*, have largely been side-stepped and left behind. But as the public success and controversy of our project proves, these are things that really matter to people outside if not in the academy.

At the same time *Redcrosse* uncovers and responds to some of the most implicitly important but also occluded questions relating to the study of English literature and culture in our time:

1. What are we to do about the intrinsic ENGLISHNESS of English Literature and religious culture in a much changed England, not to say a bewilderingly plural, global culture?

And:

2. What are we to make of the intense RELIGIOSITY of so much great English literature, in our own more diverse and secular society?

Two important creative questions grow out of these critical questions:

3. What scope is left for social and spiritual SOLIDARITY in an England that has, in many ways, outgrown the old hegemony of the Church of England establishment?[2]

And, perhaps most excitingly –

4. Could a questing and imaginative, POETIC engagement with the ultimate questions of religion create new and viable forms of cultural and religious practice in our time?

But *wait*: what might it mean to invoke English patriotism and religion positively and freshly for our contemporary world?

The story, and meaning, even the *mission* of Englishness – 'What is the country called to be, and to become?' – seem urgently important in a nation that has typically been embarrassed by imperial guilt and post-imperial decline into giving away its symbols and traditions of nationhood to unembarrassable hooligans and the far-right. Patriotism doesn't yet seem a spent force in human history, and one of the aims of *Redcrosse* is to provide a different vision of St George and St George's Day from that of forces like the British National Party. But there are reasons why I hope this story of an attempted reformation of Englishness might be of interest beyond England's borders. The critique of nationalism is so pervasive and powerful in educated academic culture that it seems important to reconnect with, not just censure and patronise, the love of one's country that is widely felt across the globe, and surely in some forms a virtue. Nor is there any way of doing this in general terms; it necessitates imaginatively reconnecting with the vivid specificities of place and culture. But to do this in one case might be exemplary for others.

Further, what we were attempting was not unrelated to the important ethical initiatives of postcolonial criticism that have been one of the major achievements of academic institutions in recent decades. For ours is a *liturgy* of Englishness; it involves confession and aims at reformation. The repentance and *metanoia* (turning around) of an old imperial culture would, presumably, be an important moral and political event in human history in general, not least because, as the best postcolonial criticism has shown, the values and the habits of the oppressors readily infiltrate what were oppressed cultures, and the culture of the oppressed insinuates itself too within the culture of the oppressors. The evolution of a chastened and repentant *former* oppressor would constitute a *different kind* of emergent culture, one which should be forearmed if not inoculated against the temptations and distortions of power.[3]

Still, there is no denying that *Redcrosse* is more about re-envisioning England, and reclaiming Englishness, than anything else. It seeks to reconnect with the concrete immediacy of life as we live it together in this country. And yet, its vision of England is not for little Englanders. It is positive, progressive and pluralist; it even opens into the infinite!

And this is where its *religious* dimension comes in. Indeed, we argue that such opening to the infinite is precisely what religion can and should do for patriotism, and that it is this that could make patriotic feeling a positive force for future good, both within and beyond England.

For precisely at this point a particular love, for one's country, shades into love itself.

It might, I hope it does, sound good theoretically, but the challenge for us was to *make it happen liturgically*, in a rite powerful enough to transform participants, intense enough to appeal to individual passions and liberal enough for anyone to join in.

*

I want to turn now to a consideration of Edmund Spenser as the poetic precedent and begetter of our project. This is one part of the story which engages with an established academic subject, though it does so in order to enrich and enable an act of civic creativity. Spenser was born around 1552, his life contemporaneous with what has been called the Elizabethan settlement. Indeed, he dedicated *The Faerie Queene* to Elizabeth: 'To the most high, mightie and magnificent empresse renovvmed for pietie, vertve and all gratiovs government Elizabeth by the grace of God Qveene of England Fravnce and Ireland and of Virginia, Defendovr of the Faith.'[4] Et cetra, et cetra: the Queen paid him a pension, and some centuries later Karl Marx called him her 'arse-licking poet'.[5] We might more positively see Spenser as *the* epic poet of Anglicanism. And if the Church of England is now all too often associated with fetes, conventional weddings and backward sexual politics, under Elizabeth the First it was a new church militant, hard-won and sometimes bloodily maintained. Everything was at stake. Church and state were united in the supremacy of the monarch. Spenser, for his part, believed that under Elizabeth a new form of poetry could be attempted which aimed at nothing less than forging a new mode of human existence. He expressly wrote *The Faerie Queene* to fashion a new man.[6]

His own life was fomented in violence. Its salient and (at least in recent years) most notorious feature was his involvement in a brutal chapter of English colonialism. He arrived in Dublin in 1580, in the wake of the suppressed Desmond rebellion. Ninety per cent of the male inhabitants of Munster had died and the survivors, Spenser observed, looked like 'anatomies of death'.[7] And yet, in *A View of the Present State of Ireland*, Spenser actually recommended starvation as a way of bringing them to heel more permanently. Nor is his poetry any refuge from such shocking violence. In 1586, Spenser acquired the manor of Kilcoman, former seat of the Desmonds. But by 1598 his Irish enemies had burnt him out and, according to Ben Jonson, he lost an infant son in the blaze. Spenser returned, destitute, to England in 1599.[8] He is buried in Westminster Abbey and his fellow poets paid tributes at his grave.

But if death thereby installed Spenser in England's Parnassus, his star has somewhat waned in recent years. *The Faerie Queene* is typically seen as too big, incoherent and remote to be read or taught effectively, and Spenser's establishment affiliations and Irish record have been major turn-offs. He's an epitome of vanishing English literature, of literature which is going from courses and becoming a more or less exclusively antiquarian interest.

The fact that, in spite of this, he refurbished and reimagined the story of St George was the germ of what became our new *Redcrosse* liturgy. But Spenser also positively stimulated our work for the following reasons:

1 His terrific self-, society- and faith-shaping ambition for poetry *which could bring new inspiration, energy and confidence to poets and writers in the present, at the same time as bringing creativity more powerfully to bear within value-establishing social, educational and religious contexts.*

2   His guilt
    which – precisely because it's so painfully regrettable – might force us, the English, to confront and 'own' the violent history of our society and its political, ideological and religious traditions.

3   A surprising correspondence, in England, between his original 'Anglican moment' and our own culturally pluralist moment
    where in both cases the spiritual identity of the nation is undetermined and in flux, to the effect that Spenser's creative response could – mutatis mutandis – help us respond more positively to our own predicament.

4   The provocation of his militant poetics in the context of current terrorism and counter-terrorism
    which could help us formulate and answer questions about what – if anything – is worth fighting for and the nature, scope, value and limitations of spiritual struggle.

The other major reason for responding to *The Faerie Queene* was, of course, the sheer power of the poetry as such, and I'll quote and zero in on a few of his actual stanzas directly. Spenser invented *his own* stanza: it has nine iambic lines which rhyme ababbcbcc, the first eight being pentameters while the final, ninth line is a hexameter. It is intricate and capable of elaborate emblematic effects, which are often exquisitely beautiful but equally extend to impressively ugly moments. And yet, the Spenserian stanza also moves with limpid fluency and authority, partly as it tips from a and b to c and spills into its long last line, which also marks a break and pause before the next stanza.

In other words, Spenser's stanza fuses lyric intensity with mesmerising story-telling momentum. It seems to be discovering its own story as it goes along. For all their seriousness and ambition, Spenser's lines are at the same time poetry disporting in and as itself. And that makes for an exciting indeterminacy. You're never really sure what the new life and self Spenser is aiming at is actually going to be like. *The Faerie Queene* is a truly and profoundly experimental poem. In the end, it does seem to reveal some kind of potential for poetry to remake life.

So this superannuated English poet actually presents the present with a tremendous and exciting aesthetic, ethical, political and religious challenge. And since we wanted to create a challenging rather than a conservative and self-securing liturgy, a *questing* liturgy, Spenser was a perfect fit.

Allegory has been a particular problem for Spenser in the recent, wilderness years, when, in his own country, his poetry has slipped into all but terminal obscurity – Salley Vickers and Sarah Apetrei testify below to how difficult they found it *actually to buy* a copy of *The Faerie Queene* – but even allegory didn't phase us. We moderns tend to think ourselves too sophisticated for allegory. It's at the same time too fanciful and too earnest and judgmental, too cut and dried. But Spenser expressly calls his allegory a '*dark* conceit', a thing shaded in mystery and perhaps irony which veils as much as it reveals.[9] The modern British poet Elizabeth Jennings describes the expressive potential of just such allegorical mysteriousness in 'The Counterpart': 'The intellect no crystal is but swarming/Darkness on darkness.'[10] If a formal image, far from being too clear and neat, keeps best faith with such darkness, because it is not excessively realised and so remains permeable to fundamental obscurity and mystery, then there may yet be life – even a life that we neglect to our own impoverishment and peril – in the knight with the symbol on his shield. Allegory, in the end, seemed promising to us because it communicates with mystery; and, given our liturgical purposes, because it is abstract enough to be co-owned by a large group of people – by anybody and everybody willing to go on a quest.[11] Especially because such abstraction in *The Faerie Queene* is richly communicative with life as we know it. For Spenser's legend of The Redcrosse Knight is *not* an escapist fairy tale; it really gets into the vein of things: into sexuality, extending to erotic dreams, infidelity, even the threat of gang rape; into depression (which Spenser calls despair), going so far as an extended representation of suicide, which it later provocatively relates to the temptations of transcendence.

So *The Faerie Queene* seemed to us to offer exciting potential for retelling the story of St George, now, for today's world. Much of this is to do with ambiguity, but much of it is also due to the mysteriousness of allegory married with a kind of ordinariness. Here – at last! – are some of the first, famous stanzas of Spenser's great epic:

> A gentle Knight was picking on the plaine,
>   Y cladd in mightie armes and siluer shielde,
>   Wherein old dints of deepe wounds did remaine,
>   The cruell markes of many a bloudy fielde;
>   Yet armes till that time did he neuer wield:
>   His angry steede did chide his foming bitt,
>   As much disdayning to the curbe to yield:
>   Full iolly knight he seemed, and faire did sitt,
> As one for knightly giusts and fierce encounters fitt.
>
> But on his brest a bloudie Crosse he bore,
>   The deare remembrance of his dying Lord,
>   For whose sweete sake that glorious badge he wore,
>   And dead as liuing euer him ador'd:
>   Vpon his shield the like was also scor'd,
>   For soueraine hope, which in his helpe he had:
>   Right faithfull true he was in deede and word,

> But of his cheere he did seeme too solemne sad,
> Yet nothing did he dread, but euer was ydrade.
>
> …
>
> A louely Ladie rode him faire beside,
>   Vpon a lowly Asse more white than snow,
>   Yet she much whiter, but the same did hide
>   Vnder a vele, that wimpled was full low,
>   And ouer all a black stole she did throw,
>   As one that inly mourned: so was she sad,
>   And heauie sat vpon her palfrey slow;
>   Seemed in heart some hidden care she had,
> And by her in a line a milke white lambe she lad.
>
> (Book 1, Canto 1, stanzas 1, 2, 4)

These stanzas make an engaging beginning, but they also involve us in various interpretative conundrums which I suggest irresistibly induct *us* into a spiritual quest that is comparable to that which Redcrosse is embarked on. Note, for a start, that the armour is dented but that the man within is still a virgin in arms. Indeed, the arms seem to have fought *without* the man: a strange and provoking image. Perhaps because this is St Paul's armour of faith which is not just fortifying but actually animating for the faithful? The poem moves on too quickly to decide. And we learn that his steed resists this 'gentle knight'. Because of his weakness? Because of his *gentleness*? Perhaps he doesn't fill his allegorical boots? Or is it that specifically spiritual militancy will not be served by a metaphor of knightly prowess without such strain as the angry steed expresses? Full *iolly* knight he *seemed*, we're told, and there's tension here between the fullness of his knightly jollity and the recognition that for all its fullness it could be only an appearance. We're informed that Redcrosse sits fair in his saddle, for the heroic adventures to come, but we've just been told he has trouble controlling his horse, which could, presumably, unseat him.

And there are stranger uncertainties still in the second stanza. 'But on his brest a bloudie Crosse he bore' suggests less a tabard than stigmata scored straight into the flesh, as the same image is scored into Redcrosse's shield. Then the *dying* Lord fights against the glory of knightly derring-do, threatening to undermine it. If dying is what's ultimately glorious and valuable, why strive for power and victory? In the Despair episode of the poem, this returns to haunt *The Faerie Queene*, with Despair whispering the seductions of death into Redcrosse's ear. The dying lord also emblematises a particularly grim and grievous kind of faith, a theology essentially, as Luther's was, 'of the cross'. And 'dead as liuing euer him ador'd' is a very odd line, because it's not clear to whom it refers. The Lord? Or the the knight? Either way, it's troubling. If it's the Lord, in what sense is he dead? Didn't he rise to eternal life, where he is now seated on the right hand of the father, etc.? Well, this line, where death succeeds life, as in our otherwise universal experience, seems to allow for the possibility that he too *just died*. Doubt, the concomitant of an honest faith – if the resurrection was assured then you wouldn't *need* faith – shows through, and with it the possibility of a godless universe.

But, because of the ambiguous syntax, even that doesn't exhaust the menace in the line. It could be *the knight* who is alternately dead and alive in his constant adoration of his dying Lord – dead and alive, presumably, in a metaphoric or existential sense? And this introduces new possibilities of morbidity, breathing into Spenser's poem from the outset the idea that even in the midst of life – even in the midst of *faith* – we might be essentially, spiritually dead. The light of life by this time seems a flickering and tentative thing, truly in need of the help of 'soueraine hope'. But such hope has been expressly undermined. And isn't faith, as it emerges here, somehow faith in *death*, in dying, in the dying of a dying lord? No wonder, then, that seeming 'iollity' crumbles into 'solemne' sadness.... It is a sadness animated by existential and religious dread. So, it may be true that, as the last line has it, the knight dreads no *thing* in the sense of a given monster or threat. But the lines seem haunted precisely by the dread of NOTHING, which is to say death which threatens to engulf both self and God in Spenser. As it does, presumably, in modernity and for us.

The stanza that follows this musters up more confidence in the knightly quest. 'Vpon a great aduenture he was bond… And euer as he rode, his heart did earne / To proue his puissance in battell braue'. And so on, with equal heartiness. What cuts into this is that lovely vision of a radiant lady leading a lamb, which, to some extent, recalls the sadness and humility which problematically undercut the motifs of manly quest in the early lines we've examined. Or does it? Perhaps Una, because that's our lovely lady's name, becomes an alternative avatar for such qualities, liberating the knight into less ambiguous heroism? That such strenuous militancy might be required is revealed in the following, fifth stanza that glosses Una's sadness. No ordinary girl, she's a universal princess, descended from a line of kings and queens whose kingdom traditionally encompassed the whole world but which has now been cruelly routed by an 'infernall fiend'. That's why she needs a man. And not just any man, certainly not one disabled by spiritual doubt. She needs a hero. But the dwarf who trails Redcrosse and Una, who appears in the sixth stanza, reintroduces the feeling of weakness and recalcitrance. The spectres of an adverse worldliness have not altogether been banished.

But we have hardly finished with Una yet. A formal image shining from the dark but no less enigmatic than the dark, to quote from Jennings' poem, she is not only the fairy tale princess, a daughter, a potentially desirable woman, a sexual partner or wife; she equally is Truth, and, in Spenser's and our own world of manifold possibility, especially the *unity* of truth, and in this, she might interest contemporary Muslims and readers of the Qur'an. The profound thought immanent in Spenser's Una is that the unity of truth is not some extra truth – which could always be exposed as just one truth among truths – but is personhood. And personhood exemplifies the *being* of truth as a whole different order of truthfulness. This is the great inspiration of theism. And this process whereby truth becomes not some propositional content but actually extends into the irreducible complexity of personality in Spenser's poem demonstrates how Spenser's dark conceits are in fact opposite to allegory, if by that we understand what is readily decoded into moral cliché.

But let's return to the verse. Suddenly Spenser chooses to remind us that his is not just an allegorical world with all the fresh contingency of a heavy rain shower. Some promiscuous laughter and mischievousness foreign to developing moral meanings redounds in his classical conceit of Jove pouring 'an hideous storm' into his lover's ('leman's') lap. And the disordered syntax and informality of 'eury wight to SHROWD IT did constrain' conveys a mad, ungainly scramble for cover. Ah! The susceptibility – the alacrity! – of LIFE. We are never elsewhere for long in *The Faerie Queene*. We are HERE, exploring and experimenting with the spiritual possibilities of our brief and therefore urgent material existence.

Allegory in Spenser, then, operates in a flickering, intermittent, multifarious fashion of what is always ultimately a dark conceit, one which is elegantly resonant with and expressive of just such an unsecured and experimental – now anguished, now joyously creative – spirituality as ours might be in our own doubtful, globalised and diverse present.

Spenser's Redcrosse is pellucidly etched as the Redcrosse Knight or Holiness. But he is a Christian, hopefully fighting his own demons;

he is equally an insufficiently mortified man under the sign of the cross which may be morbidly scored into his very breast; a sinner whose every breath and deed stains him further with sin. He is also a gallant knight in the service of the Faerie Queene; and he is the (renegade) lover of the semi-divine Una and the (renegade) lover of the very profane Duessa. And he is St George! an avatar of specifically English saintliness; and he is a crusader. And even the returned Christ who defeats Satan and regains paradise. He is various as any human person in short, and the various things he is arise from the number of different quests he is embarked on. And these are but aspects of or turns within the ONE quest which is the deeper, hungry thing that drives him. Because sometimes he *is* looking for a woman. But for love or for sex? The sacred Una or the profane Duessa? And then, suddenly, all the life force just drains out of him or turns against itself. Is it that, in his restlessness, he was really always just looking for death? Or then again is death just the necessary door to transcendence, with the New Jerusalem gleaming in its aperture? Or is it finally some more wordly, some specifically English apotheosis that Redcrosse is after? We find out as we go and the answers are contradictory and unexpected and, as a result, engaging to the extent that the experience of the quest may provoke us into our own analogous, necessarily treacherous search for meaning and value.

*

What I have been trying to do in the last few pages is convey something of the richly ambiguous material Spenser contributed to our project of creating a new poetic liturgy for St George's Day, and how powerfully his early modern story can still speak to us, if we read it with sufficient imaginative intensity and engagement. For those of us involved in writing the liturgy, Spenser became more or less important, as will be evident below. But for the prominent theologian

John Milbank, who came to the liturgy for the first time as a member of the Manchester congregation, Spenser seemed very important indeed, and Milbank's essay therefore offers a serious consideration of *The Faerie Queene* as well as *Redcrosse*. For now, suffice it to say that Spenser's poem reconceives the meaning and purpose of the red cross and St George in a questing narrative where a repentant Redcrosse only realises, and in a sense becomes, England's patron saint, after a whole series of errors and failures of a notably unheroic character.

This is a St George, we felt, who might be you or me.

Well, I say that, but even so, many of us remained troubled by the potentially excluding masculinity of The Redcrosse Knight, as Sarah Apetrei's testimony reveals. It may, indeed, have troubled Spenser, for in Book Three of *The Faerie Queene* he provides a female knight: Britomart.

We also felt it to be promising and suggestive that the fight with the dragon is in one sense the climax of Redcrosse's strange and surprising adventures but is also overshadowed by them and ultimately proves to be no real ending because, after a tidily narrated marriage with the heroine, Una, he's immediately obliged to leave and fight more battles, for the Faerie Queene.

For this is a heroic narrative as shapeless and promising as life itself.

When we reflected on it more deliberately, in the initial meetings which brought the writers of *Recrosse* together with our advisors in St George's House, Windsor, and in Manchester Cathedral, Spenser's version of St George seemed capable of standing for any English spiritual seeker for the following reasons:

1. Unlike, say, Christian in John Bunyan's *Pilgrim's Progress*, Redcrosse *doesn't really know where he's going*; like us perhaps, he's lost in a 'wandering wood'.

2. As we have seen, religion is mixed up with all sorts of other impulses and desires for Redcrosse, just as it surely must be in our own globalised, diverse and media-saturated late-capitalist society.

3. And if it's true that there's no real ending to the quest in Spenser, it may well also be that for us there can be no final and assured religious answer for us today. Perhaps there never can be and this is the meaning of faith, but if so the insecurity of ultimate truth is particularly evident and lived in our multiply divided, doubting present.

4. The ordinariness – even the sinfulness – of Redcrosse, and the untidiness of his quest and story, was especially suggestive for our project of attempting to reach or at least to address everybody in a penitential liturgical act.

In relation especially to this latter point, we were encouraged by the fact that Spenser, in his 'Letter to Raleigh', discloses that he imagined his knightly hero as an originally 'clownishe' young man who puts on the glorious armour of faith and is changed by it (*FQ*, p. 17). Because we were interested in exploring the potential for spiritual striving and even heroism of especially ambivalent, abashed, guilty, disreputable and (in fundamental ways) failed or failing people, like Spenser, like ourselves. For we, the English, like all other people, are a guilty people, both personally and collectively. And so we set to work on trying to recover something of Book 1 of Spenser's *The Faerie Queene* as an exciting spiritual adventure story, whose lost protagonist, questing after holiness, falls into degraded sexual fantasy, infidelity, pride, failure and suicidal despair, before attaining a weary triumph over a dragon, confirming that, among other things, he is a new and more truthful and realistic version of the ideal Englishness of St George.

Except of course that we wanted not just to recover (or remake)

Spenser's already renovated legend of the red cross and St George but to transform or *transmute* it into public ritual, into liturgy. Spenser already had quasi-liturgical ambitions for his poem, which he intended to transform English subjectivity and society at a time when they seemed still susceptible, malleable to imagination. But of course it was beyond his scope to make liturgical innovations to (the only recently established) order of service of the Anglican church, whereas to us it seemed not only possible but highly desirable and perhaps even necessary to do so. From the point of view of poetry, to explore its capacity to speak publicly for and with the social body on matters of the very deepest concern to all, rather than just addressing the private individual, or any aggregate of such individuals. From the point of view of the national church, to speak more directly to a changed nation and refresh the familiar ritual of the established service with new poetic inspiration. Insofar as the project was an academic one, prayer as language turned toward the ultimate – as something that might be of interest to us, rather than as a matter of historical anthropology – also seemed to us a very neglected subject.

Redcrosse, in a sense, returns to Cranmer's original ambition for a novel, vernacular rite of *common* prayer – the 1662 revision of Cranmer's 1549 prayer book is still in use in the current Church of England – but as creative practice. The Christian Church has since modernism played patron and host to some of the most liberated musical innovation, from Messiaen to MacMillan. Owing perhaps to a residual sense of the sanctity of the Word, it has been less friendly to literary innovation. But the sanctity of the Word can be turned round as a positive injunction to literary creativity, and that indeed is how the theologian Andrew Shanks, of course one of the architects and writers of *Redcrosse*, but also its major theological inspiration – and its accustomed celebrant! – sees it.[12] As a group, we saw liturgy, the national church and common prayer as potentially positive legacies, ideas and opportunites for contemporary scholarship and literature ambitious to have an impact on society.

In terms of storytelling, to turn the story of St George into a liturgy – a rite of common prayer – is to give it a much more material agency. It is, indeed, to make it more actively political inasmuch as it seeks an inspired solidarity and identity between an assembled group of people. *Redcrosse* takes the familiar image of St George as a musclebound aggressor that is beloved of the far-right and, following Spenser, redefines – indeed *recreates* – him in terms of a restless and questing openness, rendering him just as liable to get lost and go wrong as to skewer the dragon and triumph over his enemies. One of our inspirations here was Mark Cazalet's alterpiece in Manchester Cathedral featuring St George liberating a disconsolate dragon (see the frontispiece to this volume). Spenser's Redcrosse only finally defeats the dragon by virtue of the agency of God and we too sought to restore the *religion* to St George, whose heroism for us is defined by openness to others and the ultimate rather than by aggressive self-assertion.

And if in one sense we started with Spenser, in another we started with the notion of common prayer. It was while working on the project that the sheer *idea* of prayer that may be prayed in common by a whole nation struck me for the first time as extremely beautiful. That said, I love the Book of Common Prayer for its delicacy and dignity of phrasing. I admire it for the breadth of its religiosity, its way of marrying Catholic liturgy and Protestant theology (although Sarah Apetrei reminds us below that it was also a document and tool of exclusion, where we were looking to create an open and exclusive liturgy). I especially love the order of Evening Prayer, for the liturgical hush it achieves, which complements evening so perfectly that it involves a palpable hallowing of time, into which eternity seems to flow gently. I think here of 'The Third Collect, for Aid against All Perils':

Lighten our darkness, we beseech thee, O Lord; and by thy great mercy defend us from all perils and dangers of this night; for the love of thy only Son, our Saviour, Jesus Christ. Amen.

This invocation of Christ the Light in what may be the very moment when darkness falls or gathers around the congregation achieves, for me, a special liturgical intensity. But I think also of the Nunc Dimittis:

> Lord, now lettest thou thy servant depart in peace: according to thy word.
> For mine eyes have seen: thy salvation, Which thou hast prepared: before the face of all people;
> To be a light to lighten the Gentiles: and to be the glory of thy people Israel.
> Glory be to the Father, and to the Son: and to the Holy Ghost;
> As it was in the beginning, is now, and ever shall be: world without end. Amen.[13]

Here, too, is the light that will lighten the darkness, but, by perfect analogy, the darkness in this case is the darkness of death, about to descend gently on the aged Simeon now he has set eyes on the divine Son. As a liturgical act, the Nunc Dimittis makes peace with our mortality. No, more than that, it irradiates our mortality, and indeed death itself, with the joy of eternity. That it does so *in the evening* has a simple but highly gratifying rightness, a perfect correspondence to mortal time as we experience it, which makes it much more effective as consolation and promise.

In this way, the BCP is highly effective as liturgy, a real well of inspiration and consolation for English-speaking peoples. And yet, there are many for whom it is simply not culturally available, not really an original source, perhaps long-neglected but deeply recessed in the national psyche, as though in some limestone cave. What of them? There are some to whom the BCP cannot be given. Because they can't feel that it is theirs. Worse, because they can't but feel that it is really *someone else's*. I once heard the distinguished Australian poet Les Murray speak of the English canon as 'the enemy's literature' and the danger with the BCP is that it can't any longer be truly common, because it seems so very much to some to mark out those who already have English culture from those who don't.

The historicity of the BCP is also an ambivalent thing. The BCP is 'common' because it's old, established. And yet, its historical tone and timbre also makes it uncommon, not least uncommonly beautiful. But then even Cranmer was new once, though he kept a foot in the old religion.

The ambition inherent in the idea of common prayer, and the real achievement of the Book of Common Prayer itself, seemed to me particularly among the writers of *Redcrosse* to challenge us to attempt new forms of common prayer for the cultural present. It was clear that this would involve much more than mere translation into 'common speech'. Because, in fact, common prayer is anything but common speech; it requires language fresh and intense enough really to speak for and to our *ultimate* needs and longings. Which is why we turned to poetry and poets. You also can't just translate the BCP and expect it to do its job because the BCP is a product of its time, within which it really did achieve an impressive (if nonetheless limited and compromised) cultural breadth in blending Catholic and Protestant elements. But that historical breadth, while it may function as an inspiring precedent, can't now bind together in prayer a nation which extends to a bewildering multiculturalism. Our England isn't only not just a Protestant or an Anglican country; it's not just a *Christian* country. Indeed, it's not just a *religious* country. In at least some respects, it's highly secular. Its most urgently and confidently religious elements are perhaps 'minority faiths'. At a recent conference on religion at Cumberland Lodge (which also hosted the *Redcrosse* project and, indeed, made possible a kind of 'rehearsal' without music in the Royal Chapel in Windsor Great Park) it was observed by Andrew Taylor that not only were the most energetic delegates British Muslims, they were the only ones with the religious confidence freely to invoke and talk about God.

As I worked on the first draft of the liturgy I had the BCP open before me, and one fruit for me of the work I did on our new text was a renewed awe for its economy, precision and restrained passion. But we also sought to open up our new liturgy, and the ideas of a national church and of common prayer it was working with, beyond any establishment-mindedness, to anybody who might come along and feel inclined to join in. This revisionary impulse of course applied too – even more so – to the symbol of the red cross, which is so readily, and unfortunately, associated with crusading jingoism and, these days, strained or frustrated feelings of national and even racial superiority. A chilling example of this was its use on the cover of the Norwegian terrorist Anders Behring Breivik's self-published manifesto towards the end of 2011.

What civic religion at least potentially does is acknowledge the reality of a given historical identity in the very act of attempting to transcend it. Of course all the traditions I've been discussing themselves contain the seeds of and even the imperative for their own transcendence. The cross represents self-sacrifice, not self-assertion. The Anglican communion is a global one by now and Common Prayer is, in its inspiration, meant surely as a rite for all of God's people, not just to Land's End but the ends of the earth. Similarly St George is a *Christian saint*, one adopted in this country, but also, as Andrew Shanks explains below, in many others. Certainly not an Englishman. He is a figure meant to reconcile Christianity and military honour, but Christianity pulls against military honour, as Christ on the cross is sufficient to demonstrate. And, though it is often forgotten, George was also a martyr. Indeed, St George might best be understood as *a question*: a question of how military or worldly honour or patriotism might be reconciled with the religious values that exceed them. The crusading George is clearly a divisive one, not an icon that can do anything but offend British Muslims. Even the dragon-slayer as a crystallization of national virtue seems likely to stimulate at best defensive and at worst actively aggressive feelings of enmity. Then again, as especially our advisor the scholar-poet Graham Holderness warned us, the dragon-slayer has an archetypal power not to be underestimated or squandered. And we *do* sometimes need to kill our dragons. Christ came to bring not peace but a sword (Matthew 10.34).[14] George is the human face of the sword of Christ. And an invitation to think about what is worth fighting for and the nature of spiritual struggle. But Christ is surely less of a living sword than the Crucified? And a living sword seems in some ways an unpromising, not to say potentially psychopathic, figure for the aspirations of a nation. Surely we want more for it than that?

This is where the gender issue becomes urgent again. Of course there are female soldiers, and women (in history and doubtless now) are engaged in *spiritual* struggle just as much if not more so than men are, but to emblematize a nation as a living sword – as the crusader, as the dragon-slayer – does seem at least potentially to render it exclusively male. St George might seem to stand for me as a man, but he can't so readily stand as given for my wife or sister. There's a danger of substantially imagining the nation in terms of men and their virtues. And that not only leaves half of the population out of account, it even deforms that half of the nation it *could* represent, for no fully human male is to be or should be understood purely in terms of his maleness; no fully human male is just a dragon-slayer, crusader and a living sword. Thus St George as traditionally pictured can still only present part of my ideal self. And, in religious terms, a dubious part, for Christianity's representative man is defined less by aggression or even defensiveness than by passive suffering, less by victory than by self-sacrifice and, in worldly terms, failure.

For all these reasons, we were looking for a George more shaded, ambivalent and capacious, one who could stand for you and for me, for women as well as for men. St Paul thought that Christ could function in this way. 'There is neither Jew nor Greek, there is neither bond nor free, there is neither male nor female: for ye are all one in Christ Jesus' (Galatians 3.28). Spenser, as I've said, also provides a female knight; but we wanted something other than, or in addition to, a warrior figure: Sarah Apetrei considers the challenges of spiritual militancy in 'Fight the good fight?' below. In his establishing, title poem, 'Redcrosse', Andrew Motion imagines a shadowy figure beckoning us to follow him, and musingly asks, 'Is he a man or a woman?', before moving on quickly to a different question. Later he asks simply, 'What is he called?', before advising us quietly to 'forget that'. In this way, the problem of how this particular symbolic figure might stand for all the nation is acknowledged, and the figure of St George is sufficiently abstracted to be plausibly representative for all. The abstraction involves no weakening of poetic affect, rather the reverse: Motion's George is invested with an inscrutable charisma, a mysterious magnetism with a fair chance of drawing an engaged congregation, as one, beyond their ordinary lives and selves. The questions that surface are closed as potential distractions: 'Is he a man or a woman?' 'What is he called?' It could all too easily lead to new forms of provocation and division. I *didn't* say to *The Birmingham Post* as reported that 'St George could now be a woman', and I certainly didn't call for an alternative, 'St Georgina's Day', although I did say that if we need one at all, we need a St George who really can stand for everyone in England.

There it's said; now forget that. Follow him over the threshold. Together.

And yet – we felt that any concrete solidarity that our liturgy might achieve and enact in the moment of its sharing by a necessarily limited congregation should be mindfully, even prayerfully, opened to a larger solidarity with people beyond that congregation. We felt that the vocation of a national church involves a mission to the nation as such. This could take the form of representing the heritage of the nation to the nation, as, for example, the Prayer Book Society does, but this will be a living heritage only to those for whom it can be: the relatively small and dwindling number of communicating Anglicans in England. A more ambitious interpretation of the mission of the established church involves a sort of spiritual outreach to otherwise excluded elements of a partly secular, multicultural, multi-faith society. This is where we felt we needed to make a big, bold gesture. And we took our cue from that reredos painting in Manchester Cathedral of St George as a young black lad in an England football strip liberating a chained up and understandably disconsolate-looking dragon with bolt clippers against a background of urban deprivation and decay. As Andrew Shanks explains more fully below, the dragon in this image represents a passion for urban renewal. A political image, then. One which asks us to recognize that the 'face' of the country has changed, and asks us to embrace and even be proud of that change. A change which, after all, is as much a part of 'our' history as Agincourt or the Industrial Revolution.

Manchester was of course a centre of the Industrial Revolution and Cazalet's painting asks us to square up to the decline that followed its heyday and feel solidarity with the victims of that decline and a redeeming zeal in relation to it. The Catalan-style giants based on Cazalet's St George and the dragon which were features of our Manchester event made an extraordinary impression, peeping and looming in the various scenes which the liturgy evokes, quietly overlooking the making of the new red cross. We weren't saying St George was a black man, anymore than we were saying that we should henceforth celebrate St Georgina's Day, but we were saying, again, that we need a St George capable of standing for any group or person in England today. *Forget that.* In a sense we did. For our new liturgical text fights shy of any particular issue, attempting instead to open the congregation up to one another and to truth more generally. But I would not wish it to get too abstracted from the everyday political world. The danger is of it all becoming an essentially aesthetic, feel-good experience that soothes the bad conscience of its congregation, leaving everything unchanged. To that extent, the fact that a fifteen-foot black George leant into our liturgical epiphanies was a wholly appropriate material provocation and challenge. It asked, in (I felt) an eloquently embodied way, what this rite – this liturgical action – was going to mean beyond its own occasion and experiencing, in our bewilderingly post-imperial, multi-cultural, secularised and yet multi-faith England.

Our black George, in his sheer massiveness, in the gentle candour of his aspect, in the relaxed slightly sloping posture of his shoulders, is an impressive figure, a credible reminder of the great bulk of the population beyond those congregated who they are nonetheless struggling, spiritually and imaginatively, to embrace. Predictably, the far-right were outraged. Our liturgy was meant to be inclusive. We had, in fact, stepped out of our middle-class, liberal, academic comfort zone in ritualizing a reminted patriotism, but it all too predictably divided people on class grounds, with the *Guardian* in favour – we got a nice, sensitive write-up from Dalya Alberge on Monday the 24 January 2011 – with the *Star* and Nick Griffin's angry supporters against.[15] Nevertheless, our giant figure of England's patron saint made by the homeless really does stand against lazy, exclusive, retrograde – not to say wicked – forms of patriotism and national passion. I think, on balance, we were right to include him.

Our liturgy is *civil* religion. It is meant, potentially, to bind together all English people. In fact it will only ever reach a tiny fraction of them, but we hope that in those it does reach it will stimulate a better, more concrete idea of what such solidarity might be like, a hunger for it, a sense that it might even be achieved. But I said civil *religion*. I've indicated already that this is an inherently paradoxical thing and the paradox for us is that our liturgy of Englishness, inasmuch as it is a religious liturgy at all, must to that extent *transcend* Englishness. The English solidarity it seeks finally dissolves – or should dissolve – into the universal. St George is not only an English saint, and a liturgy for St George should reflect this. The national church is not only a national church – and if it is, then it's not really a church at all. The liturgy of the national church should always express this truth. The National Front website I mentioned earlier objected to our Manchester event by suggesting that St George's Day isn't a religious festival. But St George is a *saint*. The whole interest of St George's Day is in its exploration of what the religious and therefore universal aspiration of the English people should be. Common prayer finally belongs not just to all English men and women, but to all of God's people, ideally including all people as such, people of all colours and countries, people of all creeds and none.

*

I want now to return to the event of *Redcrosse* itself, and especially its central poetic element. As I've emphasised already, we chose to work within the traditions of a religious service, opening it up into a more adventurous quest for holiness, a new celebration of the red cross, but one dedicated not to shoring up a little England but discovering and even incarnating at least a little portion of a more open country.

As we've already seen from the discussion of the gender of St George, the poem by the former Laureate, Andrew Motion, entitled 'Redcrosse', helps to create the mysteriously ambiguous figure that the Saint presents to us today, as he beckons us to follow him:

> The greatest mystery facing us now is how to keep faith
> as we follow him over the latest threshold, into the world
>
> where everything flashes its label, and we expect to be
> getting the dirt, or at least the drift. Let me say it again.
> How to keep faith.

The Minister then leads the congregation-cum-audience around the Church, which is meant to be symbolic of the journeying contemplated and enjoined. They are led to four stations of the elements which we abstracted from Spenser's narrative. The first is the poem by Jo Shapcott, 'What the Forest Said', remembering the Wandering Wood where Redcrosse and Una get lost where we left them at the beginning of Book 1 of *The Faerie Queene*, and it is meant to speak to the disorientation, the bewilderment, but also the creativity of getting lost, its perils *and* its promise, its inextricable involvement in a life that is truly questing:

> Just head for the bower at the heart, don't think
> cave, or error, past or present. By now
> you'll want to be lost, so don't glance back
>
> down the trails to notice how different it all
> looks in reverse: how the aspen, the oak
> and the poplar turn, in a twist, to poplar, oak, aspen.
>
> Have the trees moved? Or is it you?

Next is 'Air: A Psalm of Many Voices' by Andrew Shanks, evoking the simultaneously treacherous and thrilling ambivalence of truth.

'Listen to the silent trouble in the air: / the hidden hubbub of your neighbours' babbled prayers'.

And murmuring, beneath the proud world's steamy din:
'Why? *Why* do I do this? I've no idea!'

Or, in the stillness of the giant's pit:
'Here – craving your forgiveness – I despair.'

Until, at length, somewhere a key creaks in a lock:
and then – fresh oxygen (thank God) floods in.

'Breathe freely now!
The "God" you thought you knew – that *wasn't* God.'

The God of *Redcrosse* is expressly 'the unknown God', and the liturgy initiates and embraces an infinite communal searching for that God, who is beyond all winning and having, beyond possession by any individual or group or tradition. In a sense, *Redcrosse* seeks to achieve a new mystical Englishness in which we can all participate freely. My own poem, 'The Fire Sermon', is written in Spenserian stanzas, and brings us into the dragon's mouth. It also, I hope, resonates with Spenser inasmuch as here desire is complexly sexual and religious; this George's love of his lady is mysteriously also his love of God. I wanted to write something that was responsive to contemporary conditions, and thus the George here is a black George inspired by Cazalet's painting and the Manchester giants, but it is the dragon who is speaking:

> My way of flame has touched your heart and face
>   With love, divorce and infidelity,
>   With this girl's glance, and with that boy's grace,
>   With glamour, power and celebrity.
>   At times from dragons you do turn and flee,

> But you have learned when you my kin must slay
> And you know now when you must set us free
> And when to soothe and stroke and make us tame
> And when to mount and ride and set the heavens aflame!

At the end of the poem, in truncated lines, this gracious dragon prophesies that George will see his last agony

> As lineaments of her face divine,
> And struggle will seem an ecstasy,
> Failure a thronging diamond mine

– and according to the last, Alexandrine line, 'The gift of this knowledge' will be 'the gift of the courage to die'.

But it is water that quenches the fire, and it is water rather than his own strength which in Spenser baptises, heals and sustains St George in his fight. Michael Symmons Roberts' 'Water Song' is about the element of water, England's waterways, and also that greater body of water which cradles and extends beyond England, Scotland and Ireland. The poem ends with the river's speaking of George's battle-weary contemplation of the sea as a glimpse into the infinite:

> He gazed along the line of my descent:
>
> from spring to pool, from tributary
> to river, estuary to shallows,
> out towards the glorious, the terrifying sea.

And here it is that civic liturgy opens into the universality of religion proper.

As I hope will have been clear, these poems attempt in context to interpolate the audience – male or female, whoever they may be – into the position of the St George that the overall work works to present. The liturgical elements I have not much commented on, but which of course are printed in the full text of the liturgy given at the end of this book, are crucial to making the story truly participatory, owned and involving. They include acts of repentance and absolution meant to address individual guilt, but resonate with national guilt; it is here that we took the stain on Spenser of his Irish record as a reminder of the collective English guilt we all share in, guilt accruing through our long history to the present. At the end of the event, a line from one of the collects resounds in the musical setting by Tim Garland: 'Make manifest, the openness that will unite us all at last.' The music meditatively recapitulates the words of the four poetic 'sermons' encountered along the way by the questing Georges of the congregation.

This music plays as the liturgy reaches its centre of gravity and climax: the remaking of the red cross by the congregation. This is meant to be refashioned – *reformed* – not in a spirit of nostalgia, and still less in a mood of defensive exclusivity, but rather as a living, flourishing thing. It is made out of that other symbol of England which is the red rose; you will recall that everyone attending the event is given a red rose upon arrival. The shared cross of many roses emphasises the openness of the participants' solidarity with one another. And if the cross in part symbolises the death of self and selfishness necessary to a truly questing and religious life – a life like St George's or even Christ's, dedicated not to self but truth – the *flowering* cross is meant to stand for the joy and fulfilment of living that life together in England. The participants are asked to give their symbolic roses to the person who comes to collect them, infusing them as they do with their own particular wish or prayer for themselves or the country. And they are asked to observe that those making the rosy cross on their behalf are the same four who spoke the elemental poems. This is to symbolise that any shared solidarity and flourishing are premised on our shared life in the body.

All Wood, and air, and fire, and water
drawn together and quartered
by blood, in sign of our common life,
prayer, and our creative strife:

O, may we be one in the struggle.

The flag is raised.

The liturgy then draws to a close with the communal singing of 'Jerusalem', with its aspiration towards a spiritually transformed England.

*

The service has not, as I write this, yet been taken to Coventry Cathedral by the RSC. Our giants will travel down for it from Manchester. It will be moving, at least to me, to see our black George in the vicinity of the bombed ruins of the old cathedral. It will be moving to see him before the altar in the eye of the huge Graham Sutherland tapestry of Christ in Glory. And I know it will move me the more to turn with everybody else at the end of the service towards the great West Window – a veritable wall of glass etched with saints and angels – beyond which the wider world of England will lie as always, waiting to be rejoined.

Notes

1 See Catherine Gallagher and Stephen Greenblatt, *Practising New Historicism* (Chicago: University of Chicago Press, 2000), pp. 136–8. In their introduction to this co-authored book, Gallagher and Greenblatt nevertheless insist on the value of the separate 'individual voice' (p. 12), identifying what was originally drafted by each author, which is why I attribute this particular consideration to Greenblatt. Greenblatt returns to 'the wicked son' in the following interview with Harvey Blume: 'Stephen

Greenblatt: The Wicked Son', *Bookwire*: <www.bookwire.com/bookwire/bbr/reviews/june2001/GREENBLATTInterview.htm> (June 2001).

2 Which is not to say there's no longer any role for the C of E in English culture but rather that the part that the C of E might play is mutating from that of hegemonic religious institution to that of, as Andrew Shanks wrote in response to this essay, 'honest civil-religious broker between many different partners'.

3 For pertinent postcolonial criticism which shows how mutually self-determining and ambivalent dominant and oppressed cultures are, see for example Homi Bhabha's *Colonialism's Culture: Anthropology, Travel and Government*, **2nd** edn (London: Routledge, 2004); Elelke Boehmer's *Empire, the National, and the Postcolonial, 1890-1920: Resistance in Interaction* (Oxford: Oxford University Press, 2002); Nicholas Thomas' *Colonialism's Culture: Anthropology, Travel and Government* (Cambridge: Polity, 2004). For an interesting postcolonial take on Englishness, see Robert Young, *The Idea of English Ethnicity* (Oxford: Blackwell, 2007).

4 All references to Spenser's epic and ancillary materials are to *The Faerie Queene*, ed. Thomas P. Roche, Jr with C. Patrick O'Donnell, Jr (Harmondsworth: Penguin, 1987).

5 Karl Marx, quoted in *The Spenser Encyclopaedia*, ed. A. C. Hamilton (London: Routledge, 1991), p. 457.

6 See *FQ*, 'Letter to Raleigh', p. 15.

7 See Edmund Spenser, *A View of the Present State of Ireland*, ed. Andrew Hadfield and Willy Maley (Oxford: Blackwell, 1997).

8 For more on Spenser and Ireland, and Spenser and colonialism more generally, see the groundbreaking Patricia Coughlan ed., *Spenser and Ireland: An Interdisciplinary Perspective* (Cork: Cork University Press, 1989) and Willy Maley, *Salvaging Spenser: Colonialism, Culture and Identity* (London: Macmillan, 1997). Also see Richard A. McCabe's stimulating intervention, *Spenser's Monstrous Regiment: Elizabethan Ireland and the Poetics of Difference* (Oxford, Oxford University Press, 2002).

9 *FQ*, 'Letter to Raleigh', p. 15.

10 Elizabeth Jennings, 'The Counterpart', in *Tongues of Fire: An Anthology of Religious and Poetic Experience*, ed. Karen Armstrong (Harmondsworth: Penguin, 1987), pp. 203-4.

11 For more on this topic, see Salley Vickers' 'For Real', below.

12 Andrew Shanks, *'What Is Truth?' Towards a Theological Poetics* (London & New York: Routledge, 2001).

13 Church of England, *The Book of Common Prayer* [1662] (London: Everyman's Library, 1999).

14 Biblical references are to the Authorised Version.

15 See Andrew Shanks' essay, below.

Redcrosse *at Manchester Cathedral.* By Tony Hardy

2

For Real

Salley Vickers

When I was asked to contribute to the work of preparing a new form of liturgy for England based on Spenser's epic poem, *The Faerie Queene*, I found myself asking the question: what can an epic allegorical poem about a knight's quest for holiness possibly have to say to a twenty-first century culture in which rapid technological advance, economic uncertainty and spiritual apathy appear to be the dominant forces? And yet the idea seemed so outrageous that I considered it. The people involved in this project were all eminent in their field and, more importantly, for I am cautious with my time, people I respect: among them, three major poets, a radical and original theologian, a brilliant Shakespeare scholar. Such quality of company is not on offer every day. So, with some reservation, I accepted the invitation and prepared to re-read my Spenser.

My own university copy of *The Faerie Queene* was buried in one of a number of boxes in the store which acts as my library. It was anyway, I recalled, dog-eared and marked with (probably stupid) pencil scribble. High time to buy a new copy, I decided.

Visits to two Waterstone's produced the same answer when I asked, 'Where can I find a copy of *The Faerie Queene*?' Back came the reply on each occasion, 'It'll be in the children's section.'

The effect on me was to feel seriously provoked. One of the once-most-famed works in all of English literature had so sunk into obscurity that it was being confused with some child's story, a sparkly Disney spin-off. How dare they, I thought indignantly, hold this national treasure in such small esteem that they do not even recognise the title.

But there followed a less aggressive thought. In their understandable ignorance, those hapless Waterstone's booksellers illuminated for me the essential quality of Spenser's epic work. It *is* a fairy story. Not the glitzy Disney kind (though Disney might make a fair fist at translating *The Faerie Queene*) but the real kind: dark and disquieting, full of mystery, ambiguity, conflict, danger, betrayal; but also full of those unfashionable virtues: courage, resourcefulness, faith and hope.

Some years ago, I was a judge for the Man Booker prize and I used quite regularly to have an argument with one of my fellow judges, who in every other way I found most congenial. 'Fairy tale' was his term of abuse for any book that did not meet his standards of what he termed 'realism'. 'But', I would argue, 'you are confusing realism with naturalism.' It is, I fear, a very modern confusion.

Naturalism is most easily defined in the nineteen-fifties spate of so-called 'kitchen-sink' dramas (interestingly, these are currently being revived). And it continues in prolific, even overwhelming, contemporary expression today. Typically, nowadays, naturalism will engage with adultery, divorce, child abuse, the problems of homosexuality, racism and its close cousin colonialism, violence, class discrimination, poverty and rape. It does not spend much time on the kind of contented quotidian happiness that many mortals luckily achieve, if only sporadically, because happiness or contentedness are not considered compelling copy. So naturalism will inevitably highlight the grimmer side of life.

Realism, however, is a very different beast. No less than naturalism it deals in the dark side of life; and to be sure, I am not for a moment suggesting that darkness is not a fit and worthy subject for our close attention. But it also deals with the light (by which I emphatically do not intend the lightweight). Realism does not, so to speak, finger the balance to give the impression that to accentuate the negative is somehow to be more humanly authentic. Which is, I further maintain, a moral sleight of hand, a cooking of the books, in short the false allure of what I have come to term 'negative sentimentality'.

Negative sentimentality is as pernicious, arguably more so, as its sweet-toothed sister. It narrows the focus and distorts the vision. It invades our aspirations, our hopes and even, quite possibly, our actions. (There is sufficient evidence of this in the mounting statistic of recognised 'copycat' crime.) There is a moment in *Chance*, by another too-neglected writer, Joseph Conrad, when the narrator, Marlow, says, 'We are the creatures of our light literature much more than is generally supposed in a world which prides itself on being scientific and practical, and in possession of incontrovertible theories.'[1] But we are also, more pertinently today, the creatures, I would even say victims, of our dark literature and I have an idea that much of the Western world's current state of discontent is reinforced, if not actualised, by the prevailing cultural worship of the negative.

There is another dangerous feature of the allure of so-called naturalism: its claims to reproduce reality. Now reality cannot be reproduced, for reality simply is. As with the scientist observing the atomic particle, any attempt, however discreet, to observe life will, of necessity, cause a distortion. Or as Wallace Stevens puts it in his great poem, 'The Man With the Blue Guitar':

The man replied, 'Things as they are
Are changed upon the blue guitar.'

This is why, to quote another genius, 'The truest poetry is the most feigning.'[2]

Here are some big examples of the truths that emerge through 'feigning': *The Odyssey*, *The Divine Comedy*, Goethe's *Faust*, *The Tempest*. And here are two others, the book of Genesis and the Gospel of St John.

Now I think it unlikely that any Christian fundamentalist is reading this book but if any happens to be let me attempt to smother your howl of protest and explain. For I intend no disrespect. Quite the contrary.

Many years ago when I used to teach a class on myth I would ask the class to begin by trying to define what a myth is. The class would offer any number of attempts at a description and finally, with a certain, no doubt irritating, smugness, I would give them my own take on the subject: 'A myth,' I would say, 'is a story that gives us the facts.'

And 'the facts', that is the real determinants of human existence, can only, and I emphasise, *only*, be conveyed through myth, poetry or story. That is to say by means of a highly unnaturalistic realism. They call it 'art'.

Was there an historical Odysseus who fought at Troy and after many years came home to a wife who had been weaving and unpicking a tapestry all that time to stave off the unwelcome attentions of her suitors? Maybe, but if so he long ago disappeared into dust while his fictional counterpart still lives on vividly in our imaginations. Did Dante walk through Hell in the company of Virgil? Probably, yes, rather as my own father sailed with Captain Ahab on the high seas in pursuit of Moby Dick while spending five years in a German POW war camp. Is there no such reality as Mephistopheles? Are Ariel and Caliban (and Miranda and Ferdinand) not, in an important sense, 'real'?

Did the Lord God *actually* walk in a garden in the cool of the day at the beginning of time? Few of us can literally believe so but what an evocative and speaking picture of the Almighty this offers for our contemplation and reassurance: enjoying the product of his creation, nature crossed with nurture, the first garden. And what an appealing image for all of human culture the garden is (as Marvell understood in his poem of that name).

Did the Wedding at Cana *actually* take place? Who in their right mind cares? The transformation of water into wine conveys a deep truth about that remarkable Jewish radical, Jesus of Nazareth: that he had the gift of transmuting ordinary everyday experience into something marvellous, celebratory and communal (it also suggests that he was far from being the kill-joy that too many of his so-called followers have, so destructively, felt it their 'Christian' duty to be). Did Jesus *actually* rise from the dead? At the risk of offending more orthodox colleagues I don't think that matters a jot. What 'matters' is how he demonstrated, through his example, that death need not be the end, as the whole history of his long-running story testifies. Life lived as it might be, *can* be, is, his story tells us, finally stronger than death.

Wherein then, lies the 'reality' of Spenser's Redcrosse knight and how can he help us reengage with the values (covered in depth in other essays in this volume) which should properly beat at the heart of liturgy? I suggested earlier that the true genius of the poem could be found in its connection to fairy tale. And fairy tale, with its 'happy ever after' conclusions, has something in common with the Christian story (it was not for nothing that Dante called his poem *The Divine Comedy*). Yet, as in the Christian story (by which I mean the story of Jesus Christ and not his Church), fairy tales also deal in darkness and death, in violence, conflict, in the lust for power and control, in betrayal and moral ambivalence – indeed, all the ingredients espoused by modern naturalism but with none of modern naturalism's narrow insistence on attempting to mimic the real.

Fairy tales, like myths, reflect back, in dramatic form, a situation, event or process that chimes with the unconscious preoccupations of their readers or audience. In that sense, they resemble the scripts that the mind evolves, directs and produces each night when we move into a different mode of consciousness and dream. Dreams also have no truck with what is prosaically (i.e. actually) possible because they are generally engaged on more crucial projects, the dramatisation for our conscious minds of our pressing unconscious conflicts, desires and concerns. And, I would add, as a former Jungian analyst, they also offer potential unrealised solutions to those concerns.

In just this way a tale will interact with its audience, bringing unconscious concerns to a consciousness which, through the suspension of disbelief, diminishes the effects of denial and repression, militates against moral righteousness, over-intellectualisation and all the other agencies of alienation which exert their influence in our culture.

I want to suggest that one important effect of a fairy tale is to permit an encounter between a society's conscious and unconscious concerns in a form which both liberates and contains. Notions of the need for psychic reciprocity lie deeply embedded in the heart of these tales which act as host or sanctuary to the unrecognised, rejected or uncomprehended concerns of its audience the better that they might contemplate them.

This, it seems to me, must also be the essence of authentic liturgy. It is a drama, a drama in which we participate, which is utterly, and inextricably, concerned with reality but not with reality as we consciously know it. It is a reality of another order.

So what about the suitability of allegory as a liturgical model? We are not as an age sympathetic to the allegorical, or we think we are not. And yet it is a medium to which children naturally respond. I have a theory that we are only truly made happy by that which makes children happy: children are not (unless they have been made sick) made happy by money, sex or power. They are capable of being made very happy by the fall of a leaf, the sight of a duck on a pond and the listening to a song or story. They are also made happy by judicious amounts of chocolate or ice cream, which is why Jesus was so right to turn that water into wine – he knew that the pleasures of the flesh also count. And this too is affirmed by Spenser in his account of the marriage celebration of Una and Redcrosse:

> Then gan they sprinckle all the posts with wine,
> And made great feast to solemnize that day. (1.12.38)[3]

Children (and adults who have not fully forsworn that more sensible state) respond to allegory because to project into story form what is inward, and often inaccessible, or unspeakable, is a deep-seated and therapeutic human impulse. It is why in the old traditions of story-telling all inner conditions are exteriorised: as angels, gods and goddesses, spirits, dragons, fairies, witches, demons. What older cultures understood, and we, to our detriment, have forgotten, is that these are time-honoured images, which give form to intangible realities for which we have only a very impoverished (and impoverishing) conceptual language.

Here is an example of what I mean from Homer's *Odyssey*:

> Athene flashed down from the heights of Olympus, and on reaching Ithaca she took her stand on the threshold of the court in front of Odysseus's house; and to look like a visitor she assumed the appearance of a family friend, the Taphian chieftain, Mentes.[4]

Athene's presence in Ithaca is not simply a flash piece of story-telling. She is there for an important psychological purpose: to reassure and encourage Telemachus that his father is alive and needs his help:

> 'The reason for my presence here,' says Athene, 'is this. ... The gods must be hindering [your father's] return, because the good Odysseus is not dead. He must be on some distant island out at sea. I am no seer or soothsayer, but I will venture a prophecy to you which the immortal gods put into my mind. Your father will not be exiled for much longer from the land he loves so well. He will think of a way to return – he is endlessly resourceful.'[5]

This comes at the very beginning of *The Odyssey* and it is this visit from Athene, in the likeness of an old friend of his father's, which galvanises Telemachus to make enquiries after his father and to begin to deal effectively with the suitors who are plaguing him and his mother in Odysseus's absence. But what is really going on here? Or, how might we describe this scene today? I think we might say something like this, that a family friend came to pay a visit and, through reminiscence and affectionate recall of Telemachus's father, activated something of the same paternal resourcefulness in his son. The human effect is the same but the means used to describe it and its effectiveness, are very different – and I frankly prefer Homer's description. Because Homer's account adds, if implicitly, another dimension: the goddess is both the vessel of valour and, co-terminously, her numinosity is generated by the valour of the young man. The human being – we might say soul or psyche – is the crucible for the reception and recreation of the divine.

The Odyssey is not allegory and Spenser is not Homer. But his allegory acts on the psyche in a not dissimilar way. Faith, anxiety, conviction, error, courage, lust, hope, confusion, wisdom and despair are all given a physical valency. In Shakespeare's words, they are given 'a local habitation and a name'.[6]

The Redcrosse Knight, with his dented armour, his 'angry steede' (1.1.1), his often ill-directed valour, Una with her 'palfrey slow' (1.1.4) and veil of mystery, the old man who looks like wisdom (and isn't), the old man who looks holy (and is), the wandering wood, the seductive Duessa, the dragon are, if I may use a word that is in danger of being overworked, archetypal. Liturgy is ritual made sacred and ritual is nowhere without the archetypal.

As others have noted the poem is all about the necessity to bring conflicting and apparently irreconcilable elements into a new form of accord. This, above all, is an accurate description of our psyches and thus the condition that any effective liturgy must speak to. We are all, in differing measure, both Redcrosse and Una, sword and girdle, light and dark, sun and moon, conscious and unconscious, error and wisdom, reverence and sacrilege, lust and, with luck, love. We are all made up of contrariness and mutability. The 'hero' (by which I include male and female) is the one who takes on these contradictions, who owns them, who holds fast to them, so that they cease to change their shape, who does not project them onto others, or, rather, who learns it is more rewarding not to. What a fairy tale hints at, and Spenser's allegory endorses, is that we must go into the dark with, if need be, 'feminine' intuition and 'masculine' opportunism, with a certain trust if we are to find the clue to the meaning of life if life is to have meaning (and 'meaning' is by no means a foregone conclusion). Through meeting what is strange and uncouth without recourse to fear, or anyway by not giving in to it, we will find unlooked-for treasures. That is the attitude of the hero and the hero is not an antique anachronism. It is a model we need as much as we ever did, perhaps more so, today.

The heroic attitude is the attitude which permits encounter with the shadow, that is our own negativity; the heroic attitude is the attitude which accepts our own contrasexuality (for we all have a male and female side); the heroic attitude sees nature as a friend and partner and not a foe; the heroic attitude believes in the supremacy of love. The hero, in short, perceives 'otherness' as finally indispensable, as vital, even intrinsic, to the self, which to my mind is what Christianity is all about.

The heroic attitude is, of course, utterly at odds with the kind of shameful xenophobia and energetic hatred of which Andrew Shanks writes. It has nothing to do with the perverse nationalism of the BNP. To find one's own ground of meaning, whether as an individual, a community or country, is to find the ground from which to respect others' other meanings.

A true liturgy enables that endeavour by giving expression to those human values which bind but do not constrict, which support but do not control, which illuminate but do not falsely glorify, in a language which strikes resonant chords rather than seeking to clarify. It does not, as so many modern liturgies do, explain. It does not, needlessly, simplify. At its best, it creates the conditions for faith to become possible, which we know from St Paul is 'the substance of things hoped for, the evidence of things not seen.'[7]

Notes

1 Joseph Conrad, *Chance* (London: Methuen, 1916), p. 261.

2 See Wallace Stevens, 'The Man with the Blue Guitar', in Wallace Stevens, *Collected Poems* (London: Faber and Faber, 2006); William Shakespeare, *As You Like It*, in *The Norton Shakespeare*, ed. Stephen Greenblatt (W. W. Norton and Company: New York and London, 2009), 3.3.16–17.

3 Edmund Spenser, *The Faerie Queene* ed. Thomas P. Roche, Jr with C. Patrick O'Donnell, Jr (Harmondsworth: Penguin, 1987).

4 Homer, *The Odyssey*, trans. E. V. Rieu (Harmondsworth: Penguin, 1959), Book I, p. 5.

5   Ibid, p. 8.
6   Shakespeare, *A Midsummer Night's Dream*, in Greenblatt ed., 5.1.17.
7   Epistle to the Hebrews, 2.2; Authorised Version.

Andrew Shanks during Redcrosse *at St George's Chapel, Windsor.*
Copyright Doug Harding

3

A Desire for the Impossible

Andrew Shanks

Liturgy versus propaganda

This book tells of an experiment. The aim? So far as I at any rate was concerned, it was to uphold, for scrutiny, a certain impossible ideal. Hence: to ponder the conditions of that impossibility – and to consider whatever 'give' there might be, after all, in those conditions.

It was an experiment in trying to shape a form of liturgy quite unambiguously opposed, in spirit, to any propaganda.

Let me spell this out. I am using the term 'propaganda' here, in a broad sense, to mean something like: communication essentially serving, in accordance with a systematic strategy, to manipulate the behaviour of large masses of people, by appeal to unconsidered prejudice, visceral hopes and fears. To be sure, not all propaganda, so defined, need serve malign purposes. But true liturgy, as such, surely operates in the exact opposite fashion. So it confronts every sort of social manipulation with the ideal of divine justice; and seeks as best it can to cultivate the imaginative resources required for a community life of real, self-critical thoughtfulness. It may do so in all sorts of different ways, loud or quiet, stark or lavish. But whereas propaganda jumps from trigger response to trigger response, true liturgy on the contrary draws its participants into a slow movement: circling around difficult reality, attending to it closely. It never flatters, as propaganda does; never gives credence to mere wish-fulfilling fantasy. And neither does it threaten like propaganda. It gives no scope for moralistic bullying. Rather, it evokes a desire for the most astringent honesty and openness, following from the event. No previous generation has ever been so constantly exposed to sophisticated propaganda; never before, therefore, has there been such crying need for true liturgy by way of therapy.

On the one hand, the Christian gospel revelation of God incarnate in the figure of the Crucified Dissident is very much a charter for anti-propaganda liturgical experimentation. Thus, why is Jesus crucified? It is because he is a second Amos; a prophet battering, intolerably, against the manipulative injustice of the rich and powerful. He does the opposite of flatter, refutes the wish-fulfilling moral fantasies of his world. Those whom he offends resort then to a final act of supreme terroristic propaganda, in the way that they dispose of him. But with a sudden flip, a judo throw, God twists all the symbolic energy of that act against itself. He whom Pontius Pilate crucified is somehow raised again to life! All the tricks that propaganda ever worked have here, in principle, been unmasked; its ultimate vacuity displayed, all in a single concentrated image, a shining moment.

On the other hand, human nature still remains the same. And the propaganda instinct soon revives within the Church itself. Pure anti-propaganda liturgy would be the ceremonial self-offering of a community, the whole unified identity of which consisted in its members' shared experience of being shaken free from propaganda-fed prejudice. In other words: a community animated, first and foremost, by a *sheer solidarity of the shaken*, in that sense. This, though, is far too demanding an ideal ever to recruit the sort of numbers that the early Church required, in order to survive in such a hostile world. The traditional rituals of the Church are not, therefore, direct affirmations of the solidarity of the shaken. Instead, they cover over the solidarity of the shaken, the solidarity principle which immediately belongs to actual gospel truth, with other forms of solidarity, a variety of local and institutional loyalties, which are more or less bound to obscure it. Church tradition endlessly mixes surviving elements of true liturgy with what has, in practice, become mere propaganda ritual. This tradition's stories, its creedal affirmations, its imagery, only make real sense in the former context. But the propaganda spirit is a prolific brood-parasite cuckoo, planting its eggs in another's nest. And the worldly success of the Church is largely due to the radical ambiguity of the solidarity of Christians with Christians, as such: the great cuckoo intrusion which that solidarity has, to some extent, always enshrined.

Still, the question remains, what would it look like if, after all, we really did set ourselves to drive the propaganda-cuckoo away? What is described here was and is (as I see it) an experiment, in a modest way, attempting to do just that. That is to say, it is an experimental attempt at liturgy directly conceived, so far as possible, as a celebration of the sheer solidarity of the shaken; even while fully acknowledging the ultimate impossibility of such a thing, as sufficient basis in itself for any more *sustained* form of liturgical community.

The enactment of the solidarity of the shaken is, I think, precisely the actualisation of what Jesus, for his part, called the *basileia tou theou*, the reign of God. It is something towards which the confessional solidarity of Christian with Christian may well open; but which, in and through that opening, also immediately transcends the given boundaries of Christendom. Therefore it is only natural that liturgy seeking the most direct possible relationship to it will tend towards a mixture of confessional with civil religion. The liturgy of this particular experiment includes sufficient Christian-confessional elements to serve as evensong in a Church of England cathedral, but it is *first and foremost* a meditation on the vocation of 'Englishness' as a civil identity, before God. It represents what one might call a form of civil religion springing 'from below'; and, at the same time, one that is somewhat set back from any particular political campaigning context.

Much of what is commonly called 'civil religion' is by contrast essentially 'from above', inasmuch as it is a religious celebration of the basic values supposed to confer legitimacy on a particular political regime. When in the 1960s, for instance, Robert Bellah famously urged Christian theologians, and others, to attend with serious critical respect to the distinctive secular truth-potential of 'American civil religion', he meant the religiousness typically infusing the rhetoric of solemn presidential addresses and the like.[1] English cathedrals regularly host liturgical events attended by Mayors in their ceremonial chains, Lords Lieutenant with their swords, High Sheriffs; all of this is likewise civil religion 'from above'. And Bellah is surely right: to do it properly does call for thought. But this celebration of St. George was of quite a different kind. And neither was it of the same kind as the liturgies in which I have participated out of doors, on the grass verge of an approach road, at the gates of the Faslane Trident nuclear missile base, or at the gates of the Menwith Hill satellite-tracking spy base where I used regularly to go when I lived in Leeds: the civil religion of the Christian Campaign for Nuclear Disarmament. The solidarity of the shaken, simply in itself, is much too intangible a phenomenon to serve as a basis for durable community life all on its own. It may very well be mixed with confessional Christian, (or other confessional) loyalties, to give it substance. Equally, it may be mixed with patriotic loyalties to a state, as represented by its ruling establishment – what else, after all, was Bellah advocating if not in effect just such a thoughtful mixture? Or then again it may be mixed with countervailing political loyalties, to a protest movement. The Church, the State, or the Movement: each of these alike may serve to give some organized coherence to the loyalties involved. All sorts of other principles may overlap the solidarity of the shaken.

What we have attempted, however, is a form of liturgy which, to an unusual degree, sits loose to *any* of these mixtures. It is, if you like, a celebration of the way in which the solidarity of the shaken transcends the loyalty principles of Church or State or Movement; as all of these tend at times to flirt with the spirit of propaganda, which is here in principle renounced. Granted, no actual religious community could ever be sustained with anything like this liturgy as its staple diet; in that regard, it does not try to do what most liturgies do. Or, more exactly, it is an attempt to do just one of the things that all authentic liturgies do, and to do that one thing with all the potential intransigence only perhaps achievable by way of an exclusive focus on it, alone.

In the event, it turned out to be very beautiful. The music was wonderful, the balance of different elements worked well in practice. I, for one, was absolutely delighted. But the undeniable weakness of this liturgy, *as* liturgy, lies in the inevitably somewhat alienating impact of its unfamiliarity, concomitant to its deliberate one-sidedness. A good many people are, as a result, liable to find it bewildering, not something they can readily enter into, make their own. It might well be said that there are two elementary criteria for good liturgy, which are by nature always liable to be in some tension with one another. Liturgy ought in principle to be as inclusive as possible; it should invite the participation of all different sorts of people, at every level of sophistication, or lack of it. That is the first requirement. But then the second is the one to which the present experiment is primarily devoted. Namely, that liturgy should, at the same time, also be as thoughtful as possible: that it should seek to access whatever shakenness is actually around in the given environment, and channel that shakenness, so that it may, as it were, all flow together and accumulate, into a single pulsing source of energy. In this liturgy the *whole* emphasis is on looking to the demands of that second requirement. If only, indeed, it were possible for a liturgical event to achieve *both* goals in full, combining unequivocal focus on the sheer shaking-power of God's truth with perfect inclusiveness! But it is not. Very largely, it seems that liturgical inclusiveness depends upon equivocation.

Vincent Lloyd has a nice, thought-provokingly odd little formula for liturgical authenticity, in its absolute essential otherness from any sort of propaganda ritual. True liturgy, he suggests, represents the ideal of '*a practice without norms*'.[2] Its inspiration comes from outside the confines of 'normality' in the sense that 'norms' are the dictates of second nature, that is, prescriptions of an unshaken spirit. 'Norms' are the moral principles by which human herds, or gangs, are governed; they are what make for a reassuring consensus. As an exemplary form of 'practice without norms', true liturgy primordially calls such repressive reassurance into question. It is no mere reinforcement of already prevalent norms. And neither, Lloyd especially wants to stress, is it the advocacy of other potential, would-be 'supersessionary' ones. In particular, he differentiates his view from that of Catherine Pickstock on this basis.[3] Pickstock seeks, very beautifully, to celebrate the truth directly inherent in the sheer 'stammering' beauty of one particular form of liturgy, that of the old Roman rite. But Lloyd asks: how far does her argument truly escape a certain 'supersessionist' logic, a mere vindication of better norms, neo-medievalist, utopian Catholic ones, over against those now prevalent in contemporary secular culture? He accuses Pickstock of such 'supersessionism'; I am not sure how justified the charge actually is. But the question is I think at any rate worth asking. What exactly constitutes the particular sort of liturgical beauty which is identical with liturgical truth? This is not obvious. And are there not some sorts of liturgical beauty that one had better mistrust? Even, perhaps, some quite refined sorts?

True liturgy is, in principle, a type of practice without even the most beautifully dreamt-of ideal norms to orient it. For to affirm norms is to be *partisan*. In Augustinian terms, it is to dress up the *libido dominandi*, an ultimately 'earthly' will to power, all unawares as something else. Of course, all liturgy prescribes. It prescribes a set of actions; and it tends to prescribe certain words, as part of these. Also, it prescribes a mode of action: maximum prayerful attentiveness. But what it does not prescribe is any merely partisan conformity to moral norms, at the end of it. The basic imperative at work is simple, 'Think!' It may well be that in the course of saying, 'Think!' – and to that end, by way of illustration – a proper, liturgically framed sermon may also, by the by, make some suggestions as to *what* might well be thought. In practice, this cannot altogether be excluded. Yet, the point is that it will only ever do so *by the by*. The one essential purpose of liturgy is to supply raw material for shared prayerful thought: a wealth of stories, images, sacred vocabulary and poetic modes of expression. True liturgy differs fundamentally from religious ritual propaganda in the sheer freedom it allows us, to make of this raw material what we will. A true liturgical community is thus the opposite of partisan. In the strongest possible sense, it will seek to pray *on behalf of* the whole world: that is, without pretending to know what is best for others – only, fiercely attentive to grief. Propaganda rituals give partisan endorsement to norms. But the whole work of true liturgy is surely just to gather strength for such attentiveness; which amounts to the exact opposite.

Often the difference between the two remains concealed, simply consists in opposite ways of inhabiting the identical practices. We, however, have tried to bring it up to the surface of the liturgical text. One effect of this: you will see that the raw imaginative material supplied by our liturgy is notably *elemental* in character. It is organised around the themes of vegetation, air, fire and water. The liturgy is a Christian one, but in a way that pulls back from the details of gospel narrative; and although it is a celebration of the patron saint of England, it makes no reference, either, to any of the actual details of English history. All liturgy is to some extent an invocation, and evocation, of eternity. Ideally, one is meant to be caught up by it, lifted out of time and out of place.[4] That is to say: out of the ordinariness of one's ordinary routine sense of who one is, where one belongs, the course of one's life, its historic setting. Liturgy is intended to try and conjure away the associated distracting chatter of gossip and news; to reframe things, if only for a moment, without any of that. Removing the things by which we for the most part orient ourselves, it is actually designed, up to a point, to bewilder. To practise it as it is supposed to be practised is precisely to cultivate a certain disciplined tolerance for thoughtful bewilderment: beyond all norms. But while such bewildered address of the soul to eternity is one of the basic functions of liturgy in general, in *this* case it is singularly direct, because minimally mediated by familiar salvation-narrative. The ever-resilient spirit of religious propaganda depends upon such narratives; it thrives on their distortion. We have tried above all to minimise the scope for that spirit to re-intrude itself. And so, for the exceptional purposes of the present event, we have retreated. Back, towards the elemental.

In my book '*What Is Truth?*' (2001) I distinguished two opposite possibilities of religious 'pathos'.[5] One is the 'pathos of glory'. This is the pathos played upon by the spirit of propaganda – in adopting the phrase I was thinking of Martin Luther's polemic against what he calls the 'theology of glory'.[6] And the other is the *pathos of shakenness*, to which that spirit is allergic. The term 'propaganda' perhaps suggests something intrinsically somewhat vulgar and crude. But by 'pathos of glory' I intend a category that may also include the most sophisticated and truly beautiful examples of religious and other artistry. The only trouble is that where art is given over to the 'pathos of glory', it is essentially engaged in glorifying a set of ideal norms as such; and hence potentially providing means for the self-glorification of the self-professed established custodians, or insurgent champions, of those norms. The 'pathos of shakenness' is the pathos that belongs to art, or religion, grounded in an experience of all norms as such being called into question. '*What is truth*', said jesting Pilate; And would not stay for an answer.'[7] The gospel answer however is given elsewhere: in the words of Jesus to his disciples, '*I am* the way, and the truth, and the life' (John 14.6). The essential truth of faith is not the truth of a correct theory or set of opinions; it is the truth of a way of life, which to us Christians Jesus definitively represents, but which in itself is present wherever there is real Christlikeness of being, even perhaps in the complete absence of a 'correct' Christian-theoretical understanding of things. So I argued. And the essence of this truth, I further proposed, is surely nothing other than the will, so far as possible, to participate in an energetic form of community life fully opened up to the pathos of shakenness, as this is so vividly instantiated by the life of Jesus himself. I then proceeded to discuss four rather diverse poets, whose lives span some three millennia, as classic exponents of the pathos of shakenness at its sharpest, prior to the compromises inevitably imposed by any at all serious strategic commitment to actual community-building, linked to it: the prophet Amos, William Blake, Friedrich Hölderlin and Nelly Sachs.

Moreover, I at least raised the question there of what it might involve to maximise the pathos of shakenness in liturgy.

It was thanks to his having read this book of mine that Ewan Fernie originally approached me, out of the blue, to invite my participation in the present project. Might we not be able to draw on the work of Edmund Spenser, he asked, if only as a point of departure for such an attempt? True, Spenser is not by any means a poet in the same category of religious greatness as Amos, Blake, Hölderlin or Sachs. Yet if his work was only to provide a point of departure, I could see that this might not matter. And so I said yes.

At all events, Spenser's 'Redcrosse knight', the figure around whom we constructed this work, is by no means one invested with much 'pathos of glory'. As knights in shining armour go, he is really quite an inglorious, even hapless sort of Everyman. In essence: a symbol of human fallenness, thrashing about in primordial anguish. And that, in fact, is exactly what we needed. For there is a sense in which the whole dynamic of our *Redcrosse* liturgy is one of being brought up short against the constraints intrinsic to human fallenness; baulked, so to speak, at the locked gates of Eden. Thus the elementary self-contradiction of the enterprise, to try and develop a liturgy – a *liturgy*, of all things! – utterly open to the pathos of shakenness at its most disturbing; when it is so central to the very concept of liturgy that it should aim at maximum social inclusiveness, and when the one goal is so very plainly incompatible with the other: what else is that, if not to enter into the most direct confrontation with the actual reality of the Fall? Such a project is admittedly wrong-headed from the outset. As indeed the Redcrosse knight, himself, is. The inglorious wrong-headedness of the knight represents the inglorious wrong-headedness of the liturgy which ostensibly 'celebrates' him. And if the latter is at all instructive, then it can only be so by virtue of the way it fails, much as he also fails, from having aimed too fantastically high.

'Do you silly jig, who cares ...'

Ultimately, no doubt, all true liturgy may be said to combine shakennness with inclusivity; and hence, with hope. First, shakenness: a sheer apprehension of the inadequacy of all things temporal to the demands of the eternal. Then, hope: the promise of salvation, as mediated, with maximum inclusivity, through traditional sacred narratives.

To an unusual degree, however, in this liturgy the whole emphasis is laid on the initial moment of shakenness, rather than on the supervening hope. Therefore, it is essentially framed as a sustained wrestling with the ineradicable reality of 'original sin'. That is, with the condition of primordial instability which precedes any actual promise of salvation; and which then opens up towards whatever element of fresh truth may subsequently be presented in promissory form.

As a concept, 'original sin' is all too often thought of in quite abstract terms, and reduced to little more than an ill-focused, pre-emptive bit of finger-wagging puritanical reproach. But the actual truth it designates is precisely that no-one is born only as a human being *in the abstract*. Rather, we are all – according to gender, ethnicity and social status – immediately inheritors of an entire history, which in each case demands thoughtful moral appropriation. So to 'believe in' original sin is surely nothing other than to recognise our need not to be over-defensive with regard to our given social identities. Negatively, it means accepting that no norms as such are ever altogether pure. More positively, it is to believe in the perennial desirability, no matter who or what one is, of being shaken free from the limitations of sympathy intrinsic to the specific norms of one's own world. This may be by way of a warmly humorous take on those norms; it may involve self-lacerating irony; at all events, it means acknowledging, with real urgency, the simple imperatives of sheer humanity, which transcend them. And that is what this liturgy in the first instance enacts, inasmuch as, while Adam and Eve stand for original sin at its most universal, one might well say that St George here represents the Adamic nature of the English people in particular. *De profundis*: a whole nation's cry to God.

There is, though, one group within the world of contemporary British politics for whom St George means just the opposite to that. The British National Party has for some time now been campaigning for St George's Day to be a public holiday in England. Its leaders have seen the Day basically as a propaganda opportunity, a chance to promulgate their brand of white 'British' racism. Indeed, there does not seem to be much humorous warmth associated with the BNP conception of St George. No irony. No connection whatsoever with the simple imperatives of sheer humanity, transcending their sense of where authentic loyalty to 'Britain' begins and ends. In theological terms, the BNP standpoint apparently amounts to a complete implicit *denial* of original sin, inasmuch as the norms of 'British patriotism', at least, are supposed to be perfectly exempt and pure. To be sure, there is no lack of passionate, sincere, propaganda-framed hope bound up with such patriotism. But this is a sort of hope entirely devoid of what I am calling 'shakenness'.

The text of our *Redcrosse* liturgy makes no direct reference to the BNP, or to their beliefs, as such. Frankly, they would have been too easy a target: too marginal, too widely despised already. We wanted to develop something with much broader reference; a principled negation of the propaganda spirit in general, and not just of any single propaganda brand. But in Manchester, where at the time one of the three elected regional Members of the European Parliament was, as it happens, the national leader of the BNP, we did nevertheless attract their attention. And news of the forthcoming event at Manchester Cathedral actually elicited something of a torrent of hate mail from them, addressed to the Cathedral, to myself, and to Ewan.

What happened was this. A couple of years previously the BNP had staged a St George's Day rally in Exchange Square just around the corner from the Cathedral. All the pubs were closed. The flag of St George was flapping merrily atop the Cathedral tower; while down below a surly crowd milled, many of them bearing the same symbol in the breeze. Whose, then, was it? The question struck me, at that moment, very forcibly.

St George is one of the Cathedral's patron saints; along with St Mary and (the threefold, Athenian / Parisian / Syrian) St Denys. In one of the side chapels there is a modern reredos painting by Mark Cazalet, installed in 2001, which shows St George as a young black man wearing trainers, jeans and an England football shirt (see our frontispiece). Why is he black? Obviously it is to protest against the misuse of the symbol by racist groups such as the BNP. That he is in a football shirt immediately prompts the reflection that there are plenty of black players who have represented England on the football pitch, as St George represents England in the domain of myth. To the extent that the myth has any real grounding at all in history, it refers to a soldier of the Roman army in the late third or early fourth century, converted to Christianity and martyred at Lydda in Palestine. Roman soldiers were recruited from all over the Empire and transferred across it, so we really have no idea what this martyr's ethnicity was. But then, why should it matter? The painting makes no pretence of referring to ancient history. It represents St George as the symbolic embodiment of an idea, the simple idea that he has always in the first instance represented: embattled courage in the service of Christ.

The hate mailers, nevertheless, professed to be utterly outraged that we had decided to accompany our poetic *Redcrosse* liturgy in

Manchester with the simultaneous introduction of two new 15-foot-high processional giants, a George and a Dragon, based on Mark Cazalet's figures. To them, they declared, this representation of St George as a black man was an act of blasphemy.

In general, the painting is a humorous one, full of little jokes and teases; quite an unusual reredos in this regard, so that it also elicits quite a mixed response from the Cathedral community itself. The middle panel depicts three figures sat around a table: the Holy Trinity? But they are in modern dress, a man, a boy and a girl, drinking Boddington's (Manchester) beer and eating chips. The man wears a hearing aid; the boy and the girl both have tomato ketchup on their chips – alluding perhaps to the blood of the Crucified, and of the Holy Spirit–inspired martyrs? Behind them are the canals and railway bridges of the city's Castlefield district. On the right is another scene: a frenzied crowd of shoppers in a place that is partly the bottom of Market Street and partly Exchange Square. And there in the midst of them glides a cheerful monk, carrying his head under his arm, the Parisian St Denys after his martyrdom. Amongst all the greed, he alone

Reredos by Mark Cazalet, Manchester Cathedral. Photo by Tony Hardy

has his spiritual head screwed on. St George and the Dragon are on the left (they are seen better in the larger reproduction in our frontispiece). Here by contrast the background is one of dismal poverty, the Lower Broughton district as it was a few years back. A drug addict can be seen in a doorway, injecting himself; there is broken glass on the pavement, and dog shit. The Dragon is a most miserable-looking beast, in chains, which St George is slicing open with a bolt cutter. As in the conventional image where the two figures are fighting, this Dragon represents Passion. But whereas in the conventional image it is unruly Passion, needing to be subdued by cool Reason, here it is the Passion of pride in one's neighbourhood, patriotic Passion, the Passion of true faith. Why, after all, is the slum neighbourhood so grim? It is surely because such Passion is suppressed, by apathy-inducing despair. Our giant Dragon is still chained up, awaiting release. But our giant St George proudly carries his shears.

They are Spanish- or Catalan-style 'gegants'. The team that made them were mostly men from the Booth Centre for the Homeless, which is based at Manchester Cathedral, working under the direction of Paul Devereaux, an artist who once lived in Spain. Each Christmas, for several years, Paul has supervised a team from the Booth Centre making a Spanish- or Catalan-style 'Belen', an expanded nativity scene which includes the whole little town of Bethlehem, for the Cathedral. Other Manchester churches, St Luke's Longsight and St Francis Wythenshawe, have in recent years produced their own gegants, I was inspired by their example, and because I knew Paul from the Belen project, it was not difficult to organise. The results, I must say, are magnificent: at once comical, as these vast structures scurry, swaying, along on the little legs of the men inside, and yet also noble. Processing behind the congregation on its trek around the Cathedral, I felt that they fitted the mood of the 8 May 2011 event to perfection. Moreover, for a number of the men in the team that made them, the creative enterprise, as a whole, appears to have been quite a momentous experience.

Already in December 2010, anxious lest we should have put so much effort into the project and then, because of its unfamiliarity, no-one in the end would come on the actual day, I happened to mention it in passing to a journalist from the *Manchester Evening News*, who was interested. A friendly story about the making of the giants appeared there. Then however it was taken up by several other papers, among them the *Daily Star* which I guess is the tabloid of choice for a good many BNP voters. 'PC fanatics', Ross Kanuik reported, 'are to turn St George into a black man. *A group of do-gooders* said they plan to lead a procession with a black puppet of England's patron saint' (21 December 2010). About a month later they repeated the story, this time with reference to 'a collection of barmy verses'. Then the website of the BNP took up the tale, with some further fantastical embellishment: 'Mancunians are upset that the city's traditional St George's Day celebrations have been scrapped [!] and replaced by a Caribbean-style street parade [!] led by a black puppet portraying England's patron saint!'

For three months, following that, the hate mail flowed, and the telephone rants. It certainly seemed to be an organised campaign. The BNP was not doing well at the time; it had suffered electoral reverses, and different factions within the party were openly feuding with one another. But, in their hour of need, we provided them with an ideal cause, combining the three passions of racism, anti-intellectualism and anti-clericalism.

If I had to award a prize to the best piece of invective, I think that, for sheer poetic verve, it would have to go to the following effort, sent by post with a flag of St George crayoned into the background:

Shanks Manchester Traitor,

Every country has their day, the English who have lived in England for over 10 thousand years, *yes we too* do have our Country day, we happen to call our Day, 'St George's Day'.

Whether a dirty foreign shit like you likes it or not, you can not ever alter that fact. *Twist, connive, dance, lie*, you silly old fart, and grow up, and have some respect for the indigenous English people, blacks & Asians *are not* natural folk here, English are white, blacks' home is Africa. Face that fact, with some sensible *fact & truth*.

Do you silly jig, who cares,
you are a stupid ignorant Judas
and stupid old bag of EVIL.

Charles and Linda C.
English patriots.

But that was in fact fairly typical of the general tone and level of argument. Time and again, the hate-mailers told me to hang my head in shame. It was, they declared, all the fault of people like me that the Church of England was in terminal decline, as they were clear it was, and no wonder. I ought to resign, or be sacked. Or, one correspondent suggested, I should be banished to the Sahara Desert – best of all, to some place highly infested with scorpions. One day seven different people left long voicemail messages on the Cathedral's telephone system, each as if vying with the others to be the most hurtful. And so it went on. How ought one to respond? I felt that an attempt was being made to intimidate me, as it were, behind the scenes; so I decided that, at any rate, it should not be behind the scenes. I wrote an article about the experience for the Cathedral News. And then the *Independent* published a two page news article, all about how hated I was.[8]

Academic funding agencies these days are always keen that applicants should be able to demonstrate what 'impact' their research will hopefully have in the world beyond academia. This tends to be understood in quite utilitarian terms: the contribution made to the national economy. Nothing could be less *utilitarian* than true liturgy. But here, nonetheless, was our evidence of 'impact': a bulging thick file of such messages. What had begun as such a very highbrow enterprise had certainly broken out of its highbrow confines. Thus far, our liturgy had indeed achieved the open, *catholic* more-than-merely-academic impact that all liturgy, properly, does aim at.

Only – to what extent had it thereby succeeded in opening up real conversation? I am afraid that it did not, with the BNP. After the Manchester event, a review appeared on their website. A 'lady from Stockport' reported:

> I attended the St George's Service and the only word I could use to describe it is 'incomprehensible'.
>
> I honestly don't believe that anyone knew what they were supposed to be doing and Andrew Shanks came across as completely barking mad.
>
> There was no logic in the narrative, no story to tell. Even the giant puppets looked lost and forlorn as they wandered about wondering why they were there at all …
>
> I asked a few people if they understood what was going on, they all shook their heads but were afraid to say so.
>
> A ban on red, white and blue was maintained by everyone apart from myself. People viewed me with a mixture of admiration and pity.
>
> What was otherwise a complete waste of time was salvaged by a hearty rendition of Jerusalem.
>
> It was a finale fit for a British National Party meeting although I expect the irony was lost on the Liberal Lovies.[9]

The use of William Blake's 'Jerusalem' as a fascist anthem is certainly, I think, rather 'ironic', in view of Blake's own politics! But then there is a good dose of irony on most occasions when 'Jerusalem' is sung. To sing it at all in a Church of England Cathedral is ironic, when one thinks of Blake's loathing for the established Church as such.

However, I do not cite this review in order to mock; on the contrary. Rather, I am sorry that the event was not lucid enough to get through even to such a sceptic. Clearly, she was bewildered because she had come expecting something quite different from what she found. She was expecting, as the heading of the article puts it, a 'White Hate Fest': a straightforward propaganda-attack on the BNP-inclined white British working class. That is the headline over the review; and she still asserts that this is what the event essentially amounted to. Therefore her bafflement is quite understandable, there being in reality no element of 'White Hate' involved whatsoever.

A second, anonymous review followed, on the BNP-related Freedom News Network website, this time however by someone altogether more assured, because untroubled, it would appear, by any actual experience of having been there; either that, or else quite astonishingly impervious to it. The article, dated 24 May 2011, featured a not very flattering photograph of me, next to the murder-in-the-cathedral headline, "Who will rid us of this troublesome priest?" And it began as follows:

> At Manchester Cathedral on May 8th, Canon Theologian, Andrew Shanks, presided over an exorcism, in music and verse, to 'kill off' [I am puzzled by the quotation marks] the indigenous English who dare to claim the St George Cross as some form of recognition of their existence.

This metaphoric genocide took the form of a walk of penance [!] around the cathedral appealing to the elements of earth and air in order to wallow in a pit of self-loathing and white guilt. The final baptism of holy water [the congregation being splashed by water from the font, prior to the reading of Michael Symmons Roberts' 'Water Song'] completed the process of atonement and participants returned to their seats confident in the knowledge that they were no longer English or white but just some obscure hue of multi-coloured Britain with no recognition as a unique, indigenous race and, therefore, no entitlement to legal representation in their own country.

This act of self-annihilation was the final solution to the problem of the English in England; kill them off by denying their right to exist in their own homeland ...[10]

One may well doubt whether any real conversation could ever be possible with the paranoid fantasist who wrote *that*. But I *am* sorry about the lady from Stockport. Even if it be in every other respect a complete success, a liturgy which merely bamboozles anyone, no matter whom, has to that extent failed.

And I also regret the consequences of the controversy, as regards opportunities for the Booth Centre men to parade the giants in public. They joined in the Manchester St George's Day parade, with a retinue of, as it happened, mostly homeless Eastern Europeans, dressed as Redcrosse knights. On the day, it appeared to be an entirely happy experience for everyone. But this, although it is billed as a Manchester event, turns out essentially in fact to be a rather wonderful local-community initiative belonging to the Miles Platting district of the city. Miles Platting is very much the sort of neighbourhood where the BNP might hope to thrive; and, after the event, the main organizer got in touch, after someone had drawn her attention to the press coverage of our project, clearly spooked by it. Then there was the question, should the giants be part of the churches' annual Whit Walk? Opinions were mixed, anxiety played a role; I could not be there myself, and did not press the issue. Next: the Manchester Day parade. But this is under close control by the Council, anxious to avoid any possibility of conflict. No banners are allowed directly identifying the participant groups; it is a celebration of civic pride, for safety's sake, at its most abstract. And a theme is decreed from on high. In 2011 it was 'Discovery'. So St George could not go *as* St George. Instead, he was given a new green jacket to wear, with binoculars and a pith helmet, thereby becoming an explorer in the jungle, accompanied by the strange new beast he had just 'discovered', and chained up. No bolt cutter. I know that at least some of the bystanders judged them by far the best exhibits on show. However, the symbolic meaning had been inverted. Various other possibilities remain for public outings; but it has been a somewhat troubling experience to encounter, in this way, some of the fear that the BNP and their sympathizers manage to generate.

Some ambiguities of St George

Of course, the BNP propaganda-appropriation of St George does not simply materialise out of nothing. There *are* aspects of the traditional cult which rather lend themselves to it. The beginnings of the cult considerably predate the Crusades: it originates in the sixth century. But from having been a martyred soldier, St George became the archetypal Christian warrior, the model of chivalry; that is what made him so popular, especially with the military ruling classes of the later Middle Ages, to whose vanity he appealed. And as such he was very readily identifiable with the whole Crusader ethos. When

Spenser depicts the Redcrosse knight / St George doing battle with three evil 'Sarazin' (Saracen) brothers, he is following a well-worn track. So too, the conventional Spanish, or Catalan, George and the Dragon 'gegants' largely serve to evoke memories of the '*Reconquista*': the long struggle to drive out the old Muslim conquerors. The BNP, in the early twenty-first century context, is keen to see itself, once again, as a band of 'Christian' warriors against perfidious Islam. Moreover, the prevailing cliché notions of St George are heavily influenced by the afterlife of Victorian and Edwardian sentimental idealisation of the Middle Ages. And this all too easily morphs into the BNP's nostalgia for the England of before mass immigration from the Commonwealth and beyond.

Note, though, some of the other things for which this protean saint historically has stood. Far from always being anti-Islamic or anti-Semitic, there have actually been times, in the folk religion of the Levant, that is, the region including Syria, Lebanon and Palestine, when the mythic St George has virtually *become* Muslim, and Jewish, as well as Christian.[11] Thus, Muslims, Jews and Christians have, all alike, honoured the figure of a green man, an icon of fertility, whom Muslims have variously called 'Al Khidr', 'Al Khadir', 'El Khudr', 'Khizr' or 'Jiryis Baqiya' (George immortal); whom Jews have identified as the prophet Elijah (Eliyahu ha Navi); and who, for Christians, has at the same time been St George ('Mar Jiryis'). The supposed tomb of St George at Lydda, the scene of his martyrdom, came to be housed in a building which was half church and half mosque, partitioned down the middle so that each community had equal access to it. Al Khidr is said by his Muslim devotees to have been an ancient pre-Islamic prophet who discovered the Fountain of Youth, or Well of Life, somewhere in the general area around Suez. Drinking from this spring, and bathing in its waters, he turned green and became immortal; repeatedly dying yet rising again, as in the cycle of the seasons. And being immortal, he is then, in the Islamic version of the myth, seen as having later on made himself manifest first to the Jews and then to the Christians, before at length becoming overtly Muslim. In all three forms he is, above all, a great healer. For example, there used to be a major shrine of St George at Bethlehem, serving as a sort of psychiatric asylum, a place associated with miraculous healings, which was visited by followers of all three religions. Seen in this context, George surely becomes, precisely, the patron saint of easy coexistence between the adherents of different religious traditions, at the level of them all sharing in the most universal human concerns.

And then, as regards the distinctive Englishness of the English St George: after all, this has by no means always been understood in aggressively ethnocentric terms. Consider for example the great 'Battle of the Flags' that erupted at Thaxted in Essex just after the First World War. The Battle of the Flags was a defining moment in the career of that remarkable, pioneering Christian Socialist, Conrad Noel (1869–1942). Noel was the vicar of Thaxted; having been appointed by the patron of the church, Daisy, Countess of Warwick, in 1910, on the strength of his already well-attested socialist radicalism. Lady Warwick had once been Edward VII's mistress, but had subsequently herself come to hold militant left-wing views; and she supposed that she was giving Noel a base for a peripatetic career, as an agitator. He, however, was also an Anglo-Catholic believer in imaginative parish ministry. And, rather than go touring the country, he immediately set out, in partnership with his wife Miriam, to convert Thaxted church itself into a centre combining fiery Socialist preaching with exemplary 'arts and crafts' excellence in liturgy: the most beautiful vestments, banners, carpets and tapestries; magnificent processions on holy days, with as many people as possible, of all ages, actively participating; Gustav Holst playing the organ; and Morris dances in the churchyard. Indeed, they succeeded in making Thaxted a national centre for Morris dancing, which it remains to the present day.

As regards flags, the church had no Union Jack in it, but the cross of St George instead. Already, this was something of an Anglo-Catholic idiosyncrasy at the time. But the idiosyncrasy was very much compounded when in 1921 Noel decided to install two others alongside the St George Cross: the Tricolour flag of the newly independent Ireland, donated to him by an Irish lady living in the parish; and a version of the international-socialist Red Flag, bearing the inscription, 'He hath made of one blood all nations'. Thaxted was a Conservative-voting town. Noel was already a highly controversial figure. Not surprisingly, this action of his infuriated some of the townspeople – although it must be said that he seems always to have retained the affectionate loyalty of his regular congregation. Immediately, a complaint was sent to the War Office. However, the officials there regretfully indicated that they had no power to intervene. A question was put to the Home Secretary in the House of Commons: what steps did the government plan to take against the open preaching of sedition at Thaxted church? Again, the same reply. And so, in frustration, the opponents called in a gang of Cambridge undergraduates to take direct action. As Noel himself records the event:

> They removed the national and international symbols and put the Union Jack in their place. Some of the devout churchgoers rallied round me and we tore up or burnt this emblem of the British Empire with all the cruel exploitation for which it stood. The undergraduates then applied to a farmer, and he helped them to erect a tall ladder reaching almost to the roof of the church, and there they placed the Union Jack. But as soon as this was done, we climbed the ladder, tore it down, and replaced our own

flags. The boys and girls were particularly brave, and burned the Union Jack. The Cambridge crowd managed to save one [charred] specimen of the imperial symbol intact, and sent it to the Bishop of Chelmsford. He wrote, severely rebuking me ...[12]

Ten years later, he remarks, some of these brawling undergraduates were to join Mosley's Blackshirts. Certainly, their devotion to the Union Jack appears to have been proto-fascist in spirit. And matters really came to a head on Empire Day, 1922. That afternoon, he goes on,

> thousands of demonstrators poured into the town and held a meeting at the Guildhall, at which one of my followers had his hat knocked off for refusing to remove it at the singing of *God Save the King*. He had a blow in the face, and was only saved by the refuge offered by a kindly Nonconformist neighbour. Shots were fired ... and things were getting lively. The crowd had left their cars and motor cycles in 'The Swan' yard, and our people, while they were busy singing *God Save the King*, cut their tyres ... There was a body of hefty ex-policemen, who had been dismissed from the force for daring to strike. They found in 'The Swan' yard a large lorry of stones with which the 'loyalist' crowd had threatened to stone the vicarage and every cottage not flying the Union Jack. It was remarkable how few cottages were displaying this symbol. These ex-policemen, who were called 'Lansbury's Lambs' [after the pacifist leader, Noel's friend, George Lansbury] drove the lorry off into a distant field, [and] emptied all its stones out ... When they returned to Thaxted, they mingled with the protestors and pretended to be their friends. They warded them off from the church, whose windows they had threatened to smash, and tried to ward them off from the vicarage. But the crowd surged up the hill ...[13]

Thanks to 'Lansbury's Lambs', the mob was in fact eventually dispersed. But every night for weeks thereafter, a vigilante team of, in Noel's phrase, 'our boys and girls' patrolled the streets and the vicarage garden to see that no further harm was done.

It was just around this time that the institution of elected parish church councils was first introduced. At Thaxted that year there was a vigorously contested election, the result of which was a council unanimously in favour of the vicar's stand. In the end, it scarcely mattered when, as had always been expected, the Chelmsford Diocesan Chancellor's Court ruled that the flags would have to be removed. Noel complied with the ruling. But, from his point of view, the real battle, for the hearts and minds of his own people, had already been won.

Thus for Noel the flag of St George was one that could readily stand in the friendliest juxtaposition to the Irish Tricolour and the Red Flag. In this, it was quite different from the Union Jack, which was he thought irredeemably associated with the ethnocentric aggression of British imperialism. As a symbol of 'merry England', the St George Cross represented an older identity, still transcending the pompous 'Britishness' of the Empire as such; an altogether more authentic form of patriotism.

Largely by virtue of association with the England football team, the flag of St George has in recent years become a good deal more popular than it was in the 1920s. Hence the BNP's perverse attempt to appropriate it as a symbol for their post-imperial, but nostalgic, fascist brand of 'Britishness'. When we decided, at the climax of our liturgy, to undertake a sacramental fabrication of the St George flag – with red roses, representing the prayers of each individual participant, gathered together into a cruciform arrangement of transparent pockets on a white sheet, to represent the common prayer of all – we certainly felt that we were working with a now somewhat tarnished symbol. But there, after all, the flag continues to fly on our Cathedral tower. And there, especially at the time of the World Cup or the European Cup, it also flaps, adorning homes and motor vehicles throughout the land. We cannot just surrender it to the fascists, without some clear challenge; any more than we can allow them possession of 'Jerusalem'. Noel's account of the Thaxted Battle of the Flags may be a bit reminiscent of P. G. Wodehouse, in tone. But it does at any rate remind us of another tradition of interpretation, deeper-rooted, and clean contrary to the fascist one. All honour to the 'red vicar'!

'The rose in the cross of the present'

Not that we were, in this, just trying to warm up the old spirit of Noel's Thaxted. Let me make it clear: although I am glad that we do not usually treat the Union Jack in church the way Americans tend to treat the Stars and Stripes, I do not myself favour *burning* it. And more generally, what Noel saw himself as standing for was 'Christian Socialism'. But 'Socialism' is always more or less the name for a propaganda-backed enterprise. It might well be what I vote for. As regards liturgy, though, I am looking for something a good deal more than just glorified back-up for my voting intentions: ideally, a whole other intensity of concern for God's levelling justice, altogether beyond any merely partisan set of loyalties.

Noel wrote two books on his understanding of Jesus as the original Christian Socialist.[14] Reading them, one can sense what a thrilling preacher he could be. But the solidarity ideal towards which these writings point, the solidarity of Christian Socialists, is by no means yet identical with what I would call the 'solidarity of the shaken'. To my mind, it is still much too partisan; too utopian; still lacking any proper critique of propagandist *impatience*.

What interests me is the question, what it would take to develop a truly effective liturgy quite unambiguously opposed, in spirit, to *any* sort of propaganda, as such. That is why I was keen to experiment with the interface between the two cultures of church liturgy and contemporary poetry. What liturgy offers to the modern poet may be entry to a whole world beyond that of poetry books and ordinary poetry readings. But what the more ambitious sorts of modern poetry offer in return to liturgy is surely, first and foremost, their embattled resistance to the sort of clichéd thinking on which propaganda thrives; their typical *indirectness*, as regards matters of theology or politics, to set against the over-hasty self-certainty of propaganda-rhetoric.

I was allotted the task of writing the text for the second of the four pilgrimage-stations in the liturgy: the one associated with the element of 'air'. (See 'Air: A Psalm of Many Voices', below.) As a priest working at a cathedral, I am constantly engaged in the public reading of psalms; therefore I chose that form. 'A Psalm of Many Voices': the air of a cathedral is forever full of other people's prayers. But the original impulse for my text actually came to me one day as I was walking down Southall Street in Manchester, a rather bleak little sloping road with industrial premises on one side and the vast wall of Strangeways Prison on the other. The teeming world the other side of the wall is completely hidden from the passer-by, yet one may well imagine the silent cries of anguish ascending into the air above.

To begin with, I situate these voices in three scenes reminiscent of *The Faerie Queene*, Book 1. First: the labyrinthine 'shadie grove' of Canto 1 and the first station, which we have just left. Then: the rowdy 'house of Pride', from Canto 4. 'Why? *Why* do I do this? I've no idea' – a tragi-comic cry, squeezed out of the bitter farce of wilful self-destruction. And following that, the 'darkesome dungeon' in the castle of the giant Orgoglio, into which Redcrosse finds himself thrown at the end of Canto 7. The poor 'wight' lies starving in this dungeon for several months on end, until at long last glorious King Arthur arrives, with the lady Una, to rescue him (Canto 8.38).

Then, after all the pent-up choking cries of anguish, there comes the response of grace:

'Breathe freely now!
The "God" you thought you knew – that *wasn't* God.'

'The "God" you thought you knew': this is the more or less distorted 'God' of propaganda ritual. That is to say, it is the only part-true 'God' of ordinary church life; the 'God' of unchallenged norms, who remains at ease with propaganda thinking in general; at worst, in Spenser's terms, the altogether false 'God' of shape-shifting Archimago and Duessa. Or, more exactly, it is the projection of what Hegel for instance analyses as *'das unglückliche Bewusstseyn'*, in English, 'the Unhappy Consciousness' or 'Unatoned State of Mind'.[15] Liturgy properly conceived as the sheer antithesis to propaganda must at least, I think, begin to *confess* its own ineradicable ambiguity, the intrinsic ambiguity of all religious utterance, as religious meaning forever shifts according to context. It is a matter of giving some liturgical expression to the old tradition of 'apophatic' or 'negative' theology, stemming back to the early sixth-century (?) writings of the Syrian Denys, otherwise known as the 'Pseudo-Dionysius' (since he adopts the persona of the Athenian Denys) or 'Dionysius the Mystic'.[16] To grow in awareness of God, this great pioneer insists, is, first of all, precisely to abandon the false 'knowledge' of God which ignores ambiguity. That simple, yet infinitely elusive, insight of Denys / Dionysius has indeed been well developed in the 'mystical' traditions of both Eastern and Western Christendom, with reference to the contemplative prayer life of private individuals. But what if we were now to start drawing on it as a source of direct inspiration also for liturgy?

The second section of the 'Psalm' gestures partly in that direction. Positive religious truth is all flare and flutter. It is like the play of sunlight on Redcrosse's armour, which, we are told right at the outset of Spenser's poem, is old and much battered; it resembles the flapping of his flag. The Red Cross upon that flag derives from the cross of Christ. Its colour represents the bloodshed of the innocent victim, Jesus or Abel. Straightaway, however, ambiguity supervenes:

'Cain, *also*, is a shepherd
herding human sheep.'

In the actual *Genesis* story it is Abel who is the shepherd, whereas Cain is a tiller of the soil. And Abel thus prefigures Jesus, the 'good shepherd'. But the notion of a whole human community behaving like a flock of sheep is surely very ambiguous! In the New Testament, of course, it is meant to signify an ethos of benign humility; yet might it not equally signify an authoritarian, or even totalitarian, regime, where the Cain-principle rules, exploiting the obedient banality of its functionaries? As a matter of actual historic fact, has not the Church itself sometimes drifted very much towards Cain-likeness, in the name of the 'good shepherd'? In England, too – on occasion, has not this happened?

'Abel's rose-red blood': the idea of making a cross, at the end of the liturgy, out of red roses was not originally mine. But the more I ponder the symbolism of the act, the more it seems good to me. Thus I think of Hegel's flamboyant little flight of fancy in the preface to his *Philosophy of Right*: 'To recognize Reason as *the rose in the cross of the present* and thereby to enjoy the present, this is the rational insight which reconciles us to the actual.'[17] (He is also reported to have repeated the key phrase here in his 1824 *Lectures on the Philosophy of Religion*.)[18] What does that mean?

It is nothing other than Hegel's lyrical formula for the type of thinking that is furthest removed from propaganda: the most painstaking, conversationally engaged and honest possible frame of mind. In fact, Hegel has two primary terms for such thinking: 'spirit' and 'reason'; *'Geist'* and *'Vernunft'*. Both terms, in his lexicon, designate what he regards, along these lines, as the very essence of the truly sacred. So, as a Christian, he conceives of *Geist / Vernunft* as the self-revealing energy of God, at work in every area of human experience, indwelling and inviting ever-closer participation, alike from each individual human soul and whole human communities. But, for him, the specific meaning of *'Vernunft'*, in particular, also derives from its opposition to merely self-enclosed *'Verstand'*, 'understanding' or 'intellect'. This is a distinction that had for some time gradually been evolving in the German philosophic tradition. *Verstand* differs from *Vernunft* in that it is much more about applying abstract logical rules than about accuracy in recognizing what is actually the case. Kept within due limits, it has its valid role. But where it overreaches itself, the drive towards *Verstand* becomes an impulse of crass intellectual impatience: the desire for a neat theory, exact ideas tidily and consistently expounded, unfortunately however curtailing real attentiveness to the world. The besetting vice of militant *Verstand*, in general, is just that it is too quick to think that it understands things when it does not. (Chapter V of the *Phenomenology of Spirit*, which is headed *'Verstand'*, parades various modes of that vice, both scientific and ethical, with a view to its remedy.) But in its over-anxious greed for immediate, supposedly 'correct' answers to fundamental moral questions, militant *Verstand* is also natural prey to propaganda. One might even say that the whole point of propaganda-ideology, as such, is to feed that hunger.

Thus, as Hegel uses the term, 'reason' – *'Vernunft'* – is above all an attitude of ideal, anti-propagandist, patient attentiveness to difficult reality. And he takes the emblem of the 'rose in the cross of the present' as a symbol for that attitude. The emblem has a history. It originates in the 'Rosicrucian' craze of the early seventeenth century: a little flurry of publications inviting Western European intellectuals to band together into an esoterically constituted initiatory brotherhood of the enlightened, for which this was to be the badge. But that is not what Hegel has in mind. Rather, he derives the image from the literature of the 'Rosicrucian' revival in mid-eighteenth century Germany. This was a politically more conservative rival to liberal Freemasonry. He has no apparent interest in the German Rosicrucians' initiatory practices. However, he *does* share their deep mistrust of the various intellectual tendencies that were eventually to culminate in the French Revolutionary Terror. For the point is that, as regards politics, authentic *Vernunft* is, above all, wary of utopian dreams: it does not come rushing in with instant, propaganda-generating prescriptions for reform or revolution. The impatience of militant *Verstand*, in general, is the overflow of *an egocentric will to control*. That is, a desire to *feel* in control of things, if only by virtue of possessing a 'correct' abstract understanding of them, for utilitarian purposes. However, the countervailing ideal patient attentiveness of true *Vernunft* springs from quite another source. And this is what the metaphor here is meant to evoke. Rather than a desire for control, the twofold ego-transcendent motivation of true *Vernunft* is

1 an infinite compassion for the suffering of other people, as represented by the cross of Christ; and

2 sheer uncalculated love of life, *amor fati*, flowering like a rose.

It is a mutual interfusing of *agape* and enjoyment; a primordial, prayerful openness to moral reality, on that simple basis.[19]

The ideal I have in mind is a form of liturgy that would really work as liturgy, hospitable to all and sundry, and yet be, without compromise, a truly faithful celebration of '*Vernunft*', or 'reason', so defined. No doubt this is impossible, in any sustained fashion. The counter-seduction of militant *Verstand*, both secular and religious, is too alluring.

Yet, even so.

Notes

1 Robert Bellah, 'Civil religion in America', in *American Civil Religion*, ed. Russell E. Richey and Donald G. Jones (New York: Harper & Row, 1974).

2 Vincent Lloyd, *The Problem with Grace: Reconfiguring Political Theology* (Stanford, CA: Stanford University Press, 2011), pp. 117, 119.

3 Ibid., pp. 113–17: referring to Catherine Pickstock, *After Writing: On the Liturgical Consummation of Philosophy* (Oxford: Blackwell, 1998).

4 For an extensive philosophic meditation on this, see for example Jean-Yves Lacoste, *Experience and the Absolute: Disputed Questions on the Humanity of Man*, trans. Mark Raftery-Skehan (New York: Fordham University Press, 2004).

5 Andrew Shanks, *'What Is Truth?' Towards a Theological Poetics* (London & New York: Routledge, 2001).

6 Martin Luther, 21st Thesis for the Heidelberg Disputation (1518): 'The "theologian of glory" calls the bad good and the good bad. The "theologian of the cross" says what a thing is.' See John Dillenberger ed., *Martin Luther: Selections* (New York: Anchor Books, 1961), p. 503.

7 Francis Bacon, *The Essayes or Counsels, Civill and Moral*, ed. Michael Kiernan (Oxford: Oxford University Press, 1985), p. 7.

8 Jonathan Brown, 'Saint George, the canon and a flood of right–wing hate', *The Independent*, 22 April 2011.

9 Martin Wingfield, 'Manchester Cathedral's "White Hate Fest"', on www.nickgriffinmep.eu (17 May 2011).

10 Anon, "Who will rid us of this troublesome priest?", www.freedomnews network.co.uk (24 May 2011).

11 Samantha Riches, *St George: Hero, Martyr and Myth* (Stroud: Sutton Publishing, 2000), pp. 33–5.

12 Conrad Noel, *Autobiography*, ed. Sidney Dark (London: J. M. Dent, 1945),

pp. 110–11. See also his earlier account: *The Battle of the Flags* (London: Labour Publishing Co., 1922). And, on Noel's life and work as a whole: Reg Groves, *Conrad Noel and the Thaxted Movement* (New York: Augustus M. Kelley, 1968), and Mark Chapman, *Liturgy, Socialism and Life: The Legacy of Conrad Noel* (London: Darton, Longman & Todd, 2001).

13 Noel, *Autobiography*, p. 112.

14 Conrad Noel, *The Life of Jesus* (London: J. M. Dent, 1937); and *Jesus the Heretic* (London: J. M. Dent, 1939).

15 The 'Unatoned State of Mind' is my proposed re-rendering: Shanks, *Hegel and Religious Faith: Divided Brain, Atoning Spirit* (London and New York: T & T Clark, 2011).

16 Pseudo-Dionysius, *The Complete Works*, English translation by Colm Luibheid (New York and Marwah: Paulist Press, 1987).

17 Hegel, *Philosophy of Right*, English translation by T. M. Knox (Oxford: Oxford University Press, 1952), p. 12.

18 Hegel, *Lectures on the Philosophy of Religion*, English translation edited by Peter C. Hodgson (Oxford: Oxford University Press, 2007), Vol. 2, p. 248, note 45: 'in order to pluck reason, the rose in the cross of the present, one must take up the cross itself.'

19 Compare the very different reading in Glenn Alexander Magee, *Hegel and the Hermetic Tradition* (Ithaca and London: Cornell University Press, 2001), pp. 247–55. Magee is admirably erudite and informative. But his whole approach to Hegel is, I think, vitiated by his inclination towards a sort of philosophic conspiracy theory. My basic reasons for disagreeing with such hostility, in general, are set out in *Hegel and Religious Faith*.

Elisabeth Dutton during Redcrosse *at Windsor.* Copyright Doug Harding

4

The Poet's Tale

Michael Symmons Roberts

Britain is very far from secular, but aspects of our religious heritage have lost their place in the culture. A couple of years ago, I was part of a group (in conjunction with the Manchester Literature Festival and Manchester Cathedral) that set up an annual 'Manchester Sermon', to allow established, highly reputed writers in other fields to apply themselves to this most neglected of literary forms. I say 'most neglected', but that's not quite true. If the sermon is a lost literary form, fatally wounded by its associations with piety, authoritarianism, preachiness and boredom, then what hope is there for liturgy?

There has, in recent years, been some interesting new thinking about liturgy. The theologian Catherine Pickstock's reading and analysis of secular and sacred liturgies, and her sense that the word represents a fundamental form of human activity, have contributed to a renewed academic interest in the form.[1] But if you tell people (trust me, I tried it while working on the *Redcrosse* project) that you're writing a new liturgy, their eyes glaze over. And that's even (perhaps especially) the case in churches, where faith in liturgies and liturgists is close to an all time low.

In recent months, English Catholic congregations have been struggling with a new translation of the Order of the Mass. I say struggling because for many mass-goers the habit of saying 'And also with you' after 'The Lord be with you' is so deeply ingrained that at least half the church still says that instead of the new 'and with your spirit'. Except, of course, for the mass-goers old enough to remember 'and with thy spirit'. From a personal point of view, this particular change comes as a relief from the rather ill-fitting chumminess of 'also with you'. But there are other aspects of the new liturgy that leave this mass-goer at least with a sense of disappointment and loss. In the creed, the new line 'we look forward to the resurrection of the dead' makes the next world sound like a summer holiday or the end of term, compared to the infinitely richer and more poetic 'we look to the resurrection of the dead', with all its resonances of a life directed and oriented by hope and faith. Likewise, the crucial words in the 'Invitation to Communion', formerly translated as 'Lord, I am not worthy to receive you' are now rendered as 'Lord, I am not worthy that you should enter under my roof'. This may indeed be more faithful to the Biblical story that lies at the root of this part of the liturgy, but its effect is to introduce an apparently random metaphor of 'self as house, or householder' that seems to come out of the blue and without any supporting field of metaphors around it. I dare say that English Catholics will get used to this new liturgy, as congregations always do with time. But the disquiet does serve to illustrate how complex and difficult liturgy can be.[2]

Why is it so difficult? In part, because it has to be spoken by so many people, so the language needs to be simple and natural enough in rhythm and meaning to allow recitation in unison, but also rich and inspiring enough to express the pain and joy and longing of the many people who will speak it. And it's also difficult because it has to stand the tests of place and time in one. It must be poetic and formal enough to be part of a profound ritual, but it must also bear repetition week after week, year after year, so that people will know it by heart and still find it robust and expressive enough to carry their hopes and fears.

As if the challenge of writing a new liturgy was not tough enough, the *Redcrosse* project set itself several more layers of difficulty. First, the new liturgy would be co-written by a team of academics, poets and celebrants. Secondly, it would try to reflect something of the poetic power and specific imagery of Spenser's *Faerie Queene*. And thirdly, perhaps most daunting of all, it would be a liturgy about Englishness, a liturgy for St George's Day, probably the most troubled and troubling day in the English church calendar.

A liturgy for St George's Day. About Englishness. Where should we start? As a poet, of course, I'm indebted to the long and rich tradition of English lyric poetry, much of it wrestling with the presence or absence of God. But when it comes to the Englishness of that tradition it seems to demand a cautious approach. We favour the war poets (like Owen and Sassoon) who were wary of nationalistic fervour over those who at times seemed to tap into it (like Brooke and Kipling). This is partly a literary judgement, on the quality of Owen and Sassoon's work, but it's also partly a reflection of contemporary English unease about nationalism. Like many English football fans, I can get caught up in the (usually anticlimactic) frenzy accompanying each new England campaign for the World Cup or European Championship. But there's something about the ubiquity of red-cross flags on bedroom windows, car aerials and tee-shirts that makes me feel uneasy. The co-opting of many of the symbols of Englishness – including St George and the red-cross flag – as symbols of the political right has contributed to a sense that England's national day is no longer a simple or straightforward feast day in the church calendar.

I was asked to join the project as one of three poets, along with Jo Shapcott and Andrew Motion, as part of a core creative team including literary critic and academic Ewan Fernie, and theologian and priest Canon Andrew Shanks. Around that group was a support and advisory network of theologians, writers and literary academics, all of whom would help us to reflect on, and wrestle with, the task of making a new liturgy for St George's Day. For me, one of the strongest aspects of the project from the outset was the prospect of the two venues where the new liturgy would be celebrated. The beautiful surroundings of St George's Chapel, Windsor Castle, felt like the very heart of a kind of Englishness – ancient and powerful and rooted in the 'establishment'. Then the brooding, dark stone of Manchester Cathedral, in post-industrial northwest England, felt like another kind of Englishness, and perhaps a more conflicted one. This sense grew when Canon Shanks told us of BNP marches (complete with St George's flags and banners) taking place in the precincts around the cathedral on St George's Day. It was important to all of us, from the first meeting, to keep in mind these two venues, these two Englands, and it served as a vivid reminder that although liturgy is a literary form, it had to work in both those contexts, for the people who came to worship at a particular place and time. It had to reflect and challenge their feelings about this English national day. And in order to do that for them, it had to do it for us first.

I came to this project with some form in the field of liturgy. Not much, but some. I had written commissioned poems over the years for use in acts of worship of various kinds. I'd collaborated with composers on 'liturgies' specially made for radio to broadcast on Good Friday, Pentecost or Christmas Day, or to respond to the 'fearful symmetry' that the ancient Christian festival of light and transformation (the Feast of the Transfiguration) falls on the same day in the calendar as Hiroshima Day. And, like most of my contemporaries,

I'd been commissioned to write various kinds of 'public' poetry, to commemorate key events. In particular, I'd been asked to write a set of elegies for Radio 4 to mark the first anniversary of the attacks of 9/11. But although all these were in some sense ritualistic, public poetry, they weren't true liturgies, designed to be spoken and experienced by whoever turned up on a particular day for a specific act of worship. The closest I'd come to that was another radio commission, for the Ascension Day service on Radio 4, broadcast live every year from the central London church of St Martin in the Fields. But even this, with its (mainly) invited audience didn't feel quite like liturgy in the raw.

So when we first met as a group, I felt like a beginner. And I came with a full set of beginner's worries. I wondered how it might be possible to hold all these disparate and complex elements in balance: the need to respond to 'Englishness', to respond to the needs of an act of Christian worship, to reflect in some way the imagery and spirit (or some of it) of Spenser's *Faerie Queene*, to create a seamless garment out of so many different textures produced by so many different writers. And perhaps hardest of all, to accomplish all these things without losing the aspiration – as with any poem – to connect with and challenge our deepest hopes and fears. To quote the American poet John Berryman: 'the sky flashes, the great sea yearns, we ourselves flash and yearn.'[3] Would we be able to reflect that?

When I was asked by the Catholic journal the *Tablet* to write a short letter about poetry to the Pope before his visit to the UK, I turned to Berryman, and used the letter as a way of reflecting on what, for me, had always been an essential relationship between poetry and faith.[4] Berryman, like other poet-heroes of mine – John Donne, William Blake, Emily Dickinson – spent his life in pursuit of this God, or being pursued, and that's what got me writing too. What could be a better fit for a poet than a religion whose founder taught through poetry. Jesus' reported words are rich in imagery, metaphor, analogy. So why – I thought, when I started going to churches – do we spend so much time trying to defuse the poetry like lethal munitions buried in the clear roads of doctrine. The point of much Christian teaching, preaching and publishing was – it seemed to me – to render the poetry of this religion into harmless prose, so the God of Christianity could be tamed, contained, predicted.

One of the qualities that drew me, slowly, towards the Catholic tradition was that much of this poetry remained unscathed, intact in the liturgy, the scripture readings, the deep and ancient rituals of the liturgical year. And yet, and yet….

In a culture disillusioned with politics, questioning consumerism, dissatisfied with the thin gruel of celebrity worship, there is a thirst for the transcendent. And most Westerners don't look to the church to slake it. I'm not simply bemoaning the rinsed-out prose of much recent liturgical writing. The issue is wider than that. Somehow, this treasure-house of human and divine poetry has come to be associated solely with legalistic language. This is not a plea to abandon doctrine, or teaching, but rather to let God (to use some of the Pope's own words) 'change us all from stone and wood into living people, in whom your love is made present and the world is transformed'.[5] This sounds like John Berryman's God. In 1970, after long bouts of illness and breakdown, the poet regained his childhood faith after a sudden encounter with what he called 'the God of rescue'.[6] Can the church become again in the West a way to meet this God? It won't be easy, but it starts with language. It starts with poetry.

As the *Redcrosse* liturgy began to develop, one of the elements that (for me) was proving most difficult to incorporate began to fade. Although one of the starting points for this group was *The Faerie Queene*, this seemed to cause more problems than it solved. How were we supposed to reflect a text most English undergraduates haven't read, let alone the rest of any imagined congregation. And as a way of talking about Englishness, Spenser's epic poem gave us problems too. After all, the Englishness in *The Faerie Queene* comes with a great deal of hubris and swagger, and a large dose of anti-Irishness, none of which we wanted to reflect in our liturgy. But there was one great gift from Spenser's work – the Redcrosse Knight himself, a figure who nodded to St George, but allowed scope beyond that figure too, in the same way that the Henry character in John Berryman's epic 'Dream Songs' could function as Berryman and not-Berryman in the same poem. Spenser gave us the liberating figure of Redcrosse, but he also gave us a set of elemental images – the wandering wood, the centrality and healing power of water, fire and air – that allowed us to see this is a liturgy of parts. And the more we thought about these elements, the more possible it seemed to write a liturgy together, but separately, that each writer could work on a separate section in his or her own poetic/liturgical voice, and that these could then form part of a larger liturgy of 'stations'. This would be a liturgy of movement, of journey, enacted within the chapel or cathedral or church. This would be a questing liturgy.

But in a project as complex and collaborative as this, every problem solved created a new problem in its wake. Our questing liturgy would bear the faint print of Spenser's poem but would function as a contemporary liturgy in contemporary language. And it could now, through its sense of journey and its different 'stations', accommodate the different voices and approaches of its writers. But a questing liturgy must be questing for something. And what should that something be? Some paradigm of Englishness? That seemed hopelessly vague and politically naive. A sense of spiritual fulfilment? What on earth could that mean? When the poet David Jones warned in the 1950s of the collapse of a commonly understood religious language, he used as examples the words 'wood' and 'water'.

A poet could no longer, he argued, place either word in a poem and expect readers to pick up a reference to the cross or baptism. He stressed that he was not suggesting everyone should subscribe to the Christian story, nor that these references should be primary. What Jones feared was that the roads of cultural memory had been blocked, and soon there would be no way back. He felt that anyone who cared about culture and language would lament the passing of a rich and important set of signs and symbols.[7] If he was right about this in the 1950s, then where do we stand more than half a century later? Are we, like Edward Thomas in his wonderful poem 'Old Man', 'lying in wait/For what I should, yet never can, remember'?[8]

Certainly I think David Jones' fears about words drained of meaning applies to 'spirituality'. I have no idea what that means any more. The word needs to be set aside for a while so it can regain its strength. The prospect of writing a broadly 'spiritual' liturgy wasn't so much daunting as incomprehensible. So we took the decision to make this a specifically Christian liturgy, but to make it as inclusive as possible. And the specificity, we felt, should not militate against the inclusivity. After all, the surest way to exclude everyone is to produce a liturgy so vague that no-one feels addressed or involved. But within that broad Christian framework (including Bible readings and a general structural adherence to an act of Christian worship) each individual writer had the freedom to try to respond afresh to the themes in the story of Redcrosse, the questing knight. My own section was to focus on 'Water', as a place of healing and rebirth, but also – the more I thought about it – as a potent image of England, with its rain, its becks, ghylls, streams, rivers and the seas that surround it.

Perhaps the trickiest decision was what to do about the flag. *Redcrosse* isn't called *Redcrosse* for nothing. And a liturgy isn't just about words and music. What should we do with this most powerful, but most complex, symbol of England and Englishness? The answer, it seemed to us, was not to avoid it or apologise for it. To do that would be to risk making the whole liturgy evasive and euphemistic. Instead, we moved the red cross flag to the centre, the culmination of the whole liturgy, in a ritual whereby the flag is made new by the placing of red roses (given to everyone as they enter the church) in the shape of a cross on a huge white sheet.

And so, how did it all go? Well, it was a privilege to work with such a remarkable team of writers. But did we succeed? Of course not. We set out to reclaim St George's day and the story of England, to provide a unified poetic and liturgical text that would enable anyone who knows or lives in England to feel included and permitted to celebrate that identity. To claim that we succeeded in achieving all that would be ridiculous. But as the start of something, a way forward, a lit taper that may suggest new ways of making liturgy, it certainly raised hopes. The majestic surroundings of St George's Chapel, Windsor made a wonderful showcase for the new words and music. But for me, on a grey Mancunian afternoon, it was the hushed crowds moving from station to station through the cathedral, in the footsteps of the Redcrosse Knight, that made me believe we might be on to something.

Notes

1 Catherine Pickstock, *After Writing: On the Liturgical Consummation of Theology* (Oxford: Blackwell, 1997).

2 For more on this subject, see www.romanmissal.org.uk (July 2012). See also, *The Sunday Missal: The New Translation of the Order of Mass for Sundays* (London: HarperCollins, 2012).

3 John Berryman, 'Dream Song 14', *The Dream Songs* (London: Faber and Faber, 1993).

4 Michael Symmons Roberts, 'Five Minutes With the Pope', the *Tablet*, 24 July 2010.

5 Benedict XVI's Christmas Vigil Homily, 'God Is Important, by Far the Most Important Thing in Our Lives', Vatican translation, Vatican City, 24 December 2009; for the full text, see: www.zenit.org/rssenglish-27943 (July 2012).

6 See Tom Rogers, *God of Rescue: John Berryman and Christianity* (Oxford: Peter Lang, 2011).

7 See David Jones, Preface to *The Anathemata* (London: Faber and Faber, 2010).

8 Edward Thomas, 'Old Man', *Collected Poems* (London: Faber and Faber 2004).

Redcrosse *at Manchester Cathedral.* By Tony Hardy

5

Fight the Good Fight?

Sarah Apetrei

For we wrestle not against flesh and blood, but against principalities, against powers, against the rulers of the darkness of this world, against spiritual wickedness in high places.[1]

EPHESIANS 6.12

It was with delight but a certain amount of nervousness that I accepted Ewan Fernie's invitation to act as a member of the Windsor Group which met to discuss the *Redcrosse* liturgy as it developed. I was invited to contribute as someone engaged in research on early modern religion and gender, with a wider interest in contemporary spirituality and the spiritual resources in England's literary heritage. The nervousness sprang from the mixed reactions I received from academic colleagues when I described the project. Historians tended to be perplexed and sceptical, finding the whole idea rather eccentric; theologians were far more accustomed to this sort of applied and interdisciplinary approach, but were nonetheless uncertain about such experimentation when it came to liturgy. In the end, my relationship with the project was not strictly confined to that of an academic consultant; my responses both to the poetry of the liturgy and to its inspiration, Spenser's 'Legende of the Knight of the Red Crosse, or of Holiness', were intensely personal, and became an aspect of my own pursuit of truth and spiritual solidarity. That level of engagement seemed absolutely fitting, and without wishing to make a subjective perspective too prominent, this personal involvement will naturally emerge in the reflection which follows, on the questions opened up by the liturgy about the nature of evil, about spiritual warfare, and about national and individual vocation.

Redcrosse and the dragon

The first book of *The Faerie Queene*, which inspired the liturgical and literary experiment documented in this book, is above all an allegory of spiritual warfare, though it also plays on patriotic, confessional and apocalyptic themes. Its climax is the slaying of a dragon, St George's emblem as well as that of Christian discipleship and eschatology: a symbol of victory over evil, death and the tyrannous self. In this section, I want to consider the *Redcrosse* project in the light of this central emblem, asking what it means to fight the dragon. St Paul's words in Ephesians 6.10–18 open the *Redcrosse* liturgy, and, together with imagery in the prophetic books and especially the Book of Revelation, have laid the scriptural basis for the ancient discipline of spiritual warfare. In all the main Christian traditions, and especially in the Orthodox and charismatic Protestant churches, the battle with demonic forces and temptations is an essential task of discipleship. I first experienced practices associated with spiritual conflict within the charismatic movement, which has been extraordinarily influential in English churches over the past twenty years and which shaped my upbringing and my spiritual imagination. Charismatic writers and preachers, particularly in the Pentecostal denominations, have generated a vast and lucrative industry around 'spiritual warfare', including handbooks for identifying occult forces, methods for deliverance and even prayers, or what are effectively mantras, to ward off satanic spirits. The biblical passage itself has been used for that purpose, and I recall that as a child, attending big charismatic festivals with my family, I was instructed in how *physically* to 'put on the armour' in prayer as protection from faceless evil. The Ephesians armour was not usually presented to me, as it is in Spenser's book of holiness and the *Redcrosse* liturgy, as the equipment for an heroic adventure in Christ: it was militant, but defensive, threatened.

As a result, I have had difficulty with the notion of the struggle with the demonic as an adult. Evil was so crudely objectified in certain charismatic circles – even given specific names, and sometimes gendered, as in the case of the notorious 'Jezebel spirit' which was thought to animate female leaders in their usurpation of male authority. Such 'spirits', it increasingly seemed to me, were nothing more than the demonization of those persons, ideas and behaviours which most disrupted special interest groups and religious authorities. I also became weary of hearing that professional feuds, marriage breakdowns or financial hardships were the consequences of spiritual attacks rather than unhappy circumstance or personal responsibility. Later, when teaching early modern History to undergraduates, I was required to look at the anthropological phenomenon of witch-hunting in early modern Europe and other societies, and it became apparent that this pernicious form of scapegoating was a mechanism not only for managing misfortune and exorcising conflict, but also for protecting dominant doctrines and structures. The process of defining the demonic or giving human form to the dragon, I concluded, was deeply dangerous and misguided, and ultimately tribalistic. Its effects in the modern world are nowhere more apparent than in the influential religious right in the United States, which has variously taken as its demons Communists, Freemasons, Muslims, Jews, immigrants, unruly women and homosexuals. Gender and nationalism are frequently caught up in the Western, masculinist construal of 'spiritual warfare' against the Devil, and something of this mentality can sometimes be detected, though to a lesser extent, in English Christian sensibilities.

When it came to reading Book One of Spenser's epic, in preparation for our preliminary meetings to discuss the liturgy, these experiences influenced my early reactions to the Redcrosse knight and his adventures. What strikes the modern reader most are the graphic, almost cinematic depictions of monstrosity and, indeed, the *personifications* of evil, and I began to loathe this crusading figure who gloried in his blood-soaked victories over sin. I distrusted a world where there seemed to be no compromise between absolute singularity and authenticity, and total falseness and depravity. Particularly disturbing were the feminine aspects of the demonic: the grotesque body of 'Errour', 'Halfe like a serpent horribly displaide, / But th'other halfe did womans shape retaine' – an anti-mother who suckled her 'cursed spawne' on her 'poisonous dugs' (1.1.14, 15 and 22).[2] Then of course there is the 'filthy foule old woman', Duessa, with her 'neather parts ... monstrous, misshapen'; the women who fawned on Lechery; Lucifera, queen of the House of Pride and those 'proud wemen, vain, forgetfull of their yoke' held captive in her dungeon among those who had 'mortgaged their lives to Covetise' and tyranny (1.2.40-1, 1.4.12 and 24, 1.5.50). The themes here are bitterly familiar to anyone who has studied the witchcraft trials which overwhelmingly targeted women in the period that Spenser was writing – pious maternity inverted; a leaking, animalistic body; sexual organs deformed; Eve's curse defied; nakedness exposed in ritual humiliation.[3]

It now seems banal for a female scholar to resort too quickly to gender as an interpretative tool. In the process of reflecting on *Redcrosse*, however, it was a theme which I was unable to avoid. As well as the female bodies of evil, I was haunted by the vital, heroic masculinity of St George, plunging the sword into the throat of the dragon. I suppose this was quite a predictable reaction, but I found it difficult to disengage an historical and a personal sense of the resonance of these witch stereotypes and gendered themes in responding to the text. For me, there were from the outset difficult ethical questions about what to do with this imagery, and with how far the allegory – spiritualized as it is – can truly be disembedded from the patriarchal culture which shaped it, then grafted onto a liberal modern spirituality. In translating Spenser's reifications of evil I felt we needed to account for the living links between symbols, allegorical abstraction and human experience. Historically, spiritual warfare has tragically been enacted in physical violence against human beings demonized as antichrist or as polluting in some way, and Paul's unambiguous words remain unheeded: 'for we wrestle *not against flesh and blood*, but against principalities, against powers, against the rulers of the darkness of this world, against spiritual wickedness in high places'.

As a lecturer in Ecclesiastical History, I am usually confined to telling stories about struggles between flesh and blood on a political stage. But there are other stories to be told, and cultural, religious and literary historians are increasingly interested in the inner worlds of societies and individuals: the emotions, spirituality, sexuality.[4] At some level, the perception still exists that these are soft, feminine subjects, whereas military affairs, economics and high politics are the real business of history, the masculine stuff which 'makes things happen'. Such a view is difficult to defend in the light of global events over the past decade. Religious passions have transformed our world and economies have been disrupted by fear, greed and deception.

In a rather different context, Eusebius, the father of my discipline, saw the difference between military and spiritual history in terms of masculinity:

> Other writers of history record the victories of war and trophies won from enemies, the skill of generals, and the manly bravery of soldiers, defiled with blood and with innumerable slaughters for the sake of children and country and other possessions. But our narrative of the government of God will record in ineffaceable letters the most peaceful wars waged in behalf of the peace of the soul, and will tell of men doing brave deeds for truth rather than country, and for piety rather than dearest friends. It will hand down to imperishable remembrance the discipline and the much-tried fortitude of the athletes of religion, the trophies won from demons, the victories over invisible enemies, and the crowns placed upon all their heads.[5]

In his *Ecclesiastical History*, manly courage for the sake of truth and piety (displayed in his account by both male and female martyrs) is contrasted to the 'manly bravery of soldiers' in the pursuit of material and patriotic conquest. Spiritual warfare is wholly inappropriately played out in violent physical struggle: these are distinct, even opposed, forms of warrior masculinity. This theme is also touched upon in the tenth Canto of Spenser's legend of Redcrosse, where, in the House of Holiness, divine grace ministers to the knight, newly liberated from captivity but broken in body and spirit:

> What man is he, that boasts of fleshly might,
> And vaine assurance of mortality,
> Which all so soone, as it doth come to fight,
> Against spirituall foes, yeelds by and by,
> Or from the field most cowardly doth fly?

Ne let the man ascribe it to his skill,
That thorough grace hath gained victory.
If any strength we have, it is to ill,
But all the good is Gods, both power and eke will. (1.10.1)

It is here, in a spiritually receptive rather than a crusading condition, that Redcrosse glimpses the new Jerusalem and receives the new name of '*Saint George* of mery England, the signe of victoree' (1.10.61).

St George's masculine patronage, in all its complexity, has been explored most rewardingly within the numinous and sometimes opaque discourse of Jungian analysis (see also Salley Vickers' chapter above). Interpreted in the light of archetypal dragon-slaying myths, the dragon is a figure of the 'devouring mother', which 'may connote anything secret, hidden, dark; the abyss, the world of the dead, anything that devours, seduces and poisons, that is terrifying and inescapable like fate.'[6] For Jung, heroic triumph over the dragon is a metaphor for the birth of consciousness that is the vocation of certain persons. It stands especially for the conquest of the collective psyche – the inferior dimension of human mentality which, as he saw it, inhibited the process of individual self-realization and flourishing:

> [I]f a man is a hero, he is a hero because, in the final reckoning, he did not let the monster devour him, but subdued it, not once, but many times. Victory over the collective psyche alone yields the true value .... Anyone who identifies with the collective psyche – or, in mythological terms, lets himself be devoured by the monster – and vanishes in it, attains the treasure that the dragon guards, but he does so in spite of himself and to his own greatest harm.[7]

Seen from this perspective, Jungian dragon-slaying might seem to be directly opposed to the aim of the *Redcrosse* liturgy to build solidarity.

Heroism is precisely not patriotic. However, in Jung's words, the process of individuation is one which tends towards wholeness and self-transcendence rather than isolation. Whereas extreme *individualism* is grandiose, rejecting the interests of the community and elevating one's own preferences and concerns, *individuation* 'must lead to more intense and broader collective relationships and not to isolation' through a deeper, more conscious appreciation of the human spirit; it 'does not shut one out from the world, but gathers the world to itself.'[8] This is expressed at times in explicitly Christian mystical language: individuation 'means letting Christ live in me. … If you function in your self you are not yourself – that is what you feel. You have to do it as if you were a stranger'; life is no longer one's own, 'but the life of a greater one.'[9] As part of this progress towards transcendence, individuation is directed towards inner *reunion* of masculine and feminine, of spirit and matter, of conscious and unconscious, rather than their opposition.

For Jungians, discovering the true Self, which Christians would identify as the eternal indwelling and universal Word, involves deconstruction of the false self and, crucially, of false enemies. What I have described as the demonizing tendency in nationalist and religious tribalism is the destructive consequence of the dragon's victory, of illusory security and fantasized collective identity. The Canadian feminist and Jungian analyst Marion Woodman writes of the dangers of 'concretizing' or objectifying evil, in these perplexing but suggestive terms:

> The symbolic meaning of killing as sacrifice which leads to transformation has been lost. Transformation moves energy from the unconscious to consciousness. When dragon slaying is concretized, mother becomes concrete matter, and unconsciously her children continue to worship the outworn mother because the

consciousness that would lead to transformation is not present. Without it, killing the mother only leads to bringing her back in a stronger form, since she feeds on the energy of the killer – as many an addict has discovered. In the myth, death is followed by resurrection, but in our concretized culture, there is only death.[10]

What I think this means – and it is hardly transparent when removed from its context – is that when we attempt to overcome as 'dragon-slayers' those material addictions and investments which provide false security (the authoritarian 'mother'), they will be quickly replaced by new, equally consuming and illusory securities. True transformation, Jung's true heroism, requires a conscious examination and domestication of what it is that tyrannizes over us, preventing us from encountering Christ and becoming most truly our created selves. Regeneration is to be found in this realisation. This understanding of spiritual warfare as an interior struggle is not, of course, exclusively Jungian or even exclusively Christian. In our consultation at Windsor prior to the writing of the liturgy, I was deeply struck by Monawar Hussain's exploration of the parallels between Redcrosse's journey and the Sufi battle (the 'higher jihād') with *nafs*, or the lower soul: the seat of commanding desire. The freedom offered by such a transformation through peaceful war or jihād may be expressed in the *Redcrosse* liturgy in Ewan Fernie's dragon-breathing 'Fire Sermon', and in Michael Symmons Roberts' 'Water Song':

But you have learned when you my kin must slay
And you know now when you must set us free
And when to soothe and stroke and make us tame
And when to mount and ride and set the heavens aflame!

It was George who split the dragon's throat,
who fought until his sword was blunt.

But beast fell ghost, and George fell to his knees.
He gazed along the line of my descent:

from spring to pool, from tributary
to river, estuary to shallows,
out towards the glorious, the terrifying sea.

'When all the games have stopped'

Vocation has to do with saving your soul – not by acquiring a secure position of holiness, but by learning to shed the unreality that suffocates the very life of the soul. ... Vocation is, you could say, what's left when all the games have stopped.[11]

ROWAN WILLIAMS

In the second part of this chapter, I want to ask, what's left of any sense of English national vocation? The blood-red symbol of our nationhood, the cross of passion emblazoned on white, rose to prominence as the lifted banner of the crusader; the English have stood beneath it through reformation, revolution, enlightenment and empire. It has been associated with the impulse to convert, christianize, colonize and civilize. It once signified an enduring, noble and destructive belief that England was an elect nation, called to holiness above all others.

What's left are the games.

St George's flag now flutters from the windows in council estates and well-heeled suburbs alike, during the great rugby, cricket and football World Cup tournaments, in our most public displays of patriotism. On the field are the national heroes – all male, mind you – competing for hard-won but fleeting victory. Rugby, cricket, football: these games all developed in their modern form primarily in the British Isles, and in England in particular, alongside notions of 'fair play', for which the English are still (perhaps unjustly) celebrated. St George is invoked as their patron saint, presiding anxiously over disappointment, defeat and precarious successes. It is a tribal St George, destined to be frustrated by failures of masculine performance and the faded memory of glory.

The fact that English national pride is most visibly defended by wealthy men playing ball games is a salutary reminder not only that patriotism usually takes muscular, masculine forms, but also that our patriotic heroes are 'players': performing a parody of conflict, and upon whom fantasies of victory and honour are projected. More tragically, we are knowing enough to recognise that the battles in which young men and women, not only from England but across the British Isles, sacrifice themselves (often truly heroically) are rarely fought over the higher patriotic values. Wounded by the brutal decimation of whole generations of men in the twentieth century, the British are no longer persuaded by Hollywood myths of patriotic glory; many Americans are increasingly disenchanted with their war games too. Our diplomatic stance is defensive, security-conscious, self-interested. It is a common perception that our interference in the affairs of other states is increasingly a form of economic power play, paying a very high price to support privileged interest groups. What is 'reality' in these conflicts? Is it the wealth, influence and acumen of the arms trader, or the eloquent democratic rhetoric of the politician, or the broken heart of the British/Afghan mother? While reality is the pawn of the game-players, patriotism has little purpose and offers no hope.

True vocation, in the words of a Welshman presiding over the English Church, is what's left when all the games have stopped.

There is hope to be found in the possibility that the games are stopping, that illusions are quite suddenly dissipating and scales are falling from eyes. It has become almost platitudinous to observe that our nation, and with it our world, is involved in a profound crisis that is moral and spiritual just as surely as it is financial. The period since the *Redcrosse* project was conceived has seen an extraordinary surge of outrage, principally about deception, hypocrisy and injustice in the places of power; it all accords very resonantly with the quotation from Ephesians which is part of the liturgy and the epigraph to this chapter. The central institutions of English society have been shaken, and their corruptions are being exposed. As riots inflamed London in the summer months of 2011, it struck me that this was an infection which ran from the head to the feet. When senior police officers take bribes, MPs plunder the public purse, bankers gamble away the pensions of the poor but keep a tight grip on their own profits, and the media routinely breaks the law for the sake of profit, why on earth are we surprised by the lawless greed of the mob? Who is there with the authority to tell us that looting is wrong? As Andrew Motion and the co-writers of the liturgy put it,

> *The greatest mystery facing us now is how to keep faith*
> *as we follow him over the latest threshold, into the world*
> *where everything flashes its label, and we expect to be*
> *getting the dirt, or at least the drift.*
>
> *O God, we have gone wrong,*
> *And wandered like lost sheep.*
> *We heard your call,*
> *It touched our hearts, but surface things seduced us.*
> *Spoilt, then, we present ourselves*
> *Before your face, and beg to be forgiven.*

Of course, every generation has lamented loudly over moral decline and corruption, and we should not imagine that humanity is any more degraded than it ever has been. (Original sin, I've heard it said, is the most plausible of Christian doctrines.) But more than any other kind of national soul-searching that I can remember – more than the mourning of Diana, or the shock of 9/11, or the protests against the Iraq war – this involves each English, and one might say every Western, woman and man. The way we have constructed ourselves and our lifestyles is basically illusory, founded on the self-deception of unsustainable credit and unmanageable debt. Outrage is *justly* and, I believe, must *increasingly* be poured out on the institutions which were most aggressive in promoting this grotesque deception. And yet, there must also be a groundswell of outrage about how we have deceived ourselves, plunging, greedily, headfirst into an ocean of unreality. The dragon is not an exterior demon; if we only scapegoat the bankers and leave unexamined the underlying distortions in our sense of entitlement and in the emotional and social pressures which hound us, and in our delusions of comfort, we will not exorcise anything. We are all implicated in the reckless, devouring collective unconscious, the plundering of resources for imagined security, and we – I – must wake up from the dream. As Rowan Williams explains his essay on 'Vocation', quoted above:

> Crises occur at those points where we see how unreality, our selfish, self-protecting illusions, our struggles for cheap security, block the way to our answering the call to be. To live like this, to nurture and develop this image of myself, may be safe, but it isn't true: insofar as it's unreal it's un-Godly. God cannot reach me if I'm not there.
>
> The crisis comes when we put the question, 'What am I denying, what am I refusing to see in myself? What am I trying to avoid?' This is where we have to begin really to attend to ourselves and to the world around, to find out what is true and what is false in us.[12]

The best that we can patriotically hope for in these troubled times, and it is not a hollow hope, is that we might begin to see more clearly what is true and what is false in us, and perhaps learn something about our painful calling from unreality. Our nation's flag, a bold and uncompromising cross of red on the void of white, demands the truth: for where there is truth, there is God.

What is this England?
We have a patron saint.
What does he stand for?
We have a flag.

Sometimes it speaks of sporting passion. Sometimes it speaks of pomp. Sometimes it speaks of grief, at memories of war. Sometimes it speaks of vicious hatred. But when it flies upon this church it speaks of something else. (Redcrosse)

Stepping out on to the platform at Windsor train station in April 2010, for the first of our meetings to discuss the *Redcrosse* liturgy, I suddenly felt an unwelcome sense of being part of an *establishment*. Cowed by the overpriced boutique shops, the patriotic merchandise and the towering castle walls, I made my way past armed guards to seek out the gracious medieval room at the College of St George where I, an Oxford church historian, was to meet a cathedral canon, a tutor from Eton, and numerous other distinguished clergymen, writers and academics. It was unnerving, partly because I am not accustomed to thinking of myself as occupying a place within the establishment, and partly because it caused me to wonder: could we, the privileged insiders, secure behind those ramparts, really have anything to say to the England beyond? Did any of us have the first clue what it meant to feel powerless and resentful, threatened and defensive? It now seems clear to me that the location and the composition of the group were significant, indicating that, in the words of the St George's House brochure, there is at the very heart of the establishment a desire 'to nurture Wisdom and open up the possibility of a different and better world.' The Wisdom that is envisaged is 'forward-looking and free from contemporary idols': it is the capacity to 'think the unthinkable' for the sake of the spiritual transformation of society. I can think of no better characterization of dragon-slaying. And there were other dimensions to the project, of course, in particular the Manchester group, with its contributions from homeless people as well as local poets and artists.

The macrocosm is contained in the microcosm: we are all involved with one another, and national myths play out in personal narratives, as well as vice versa. In Andrew Motion's words in the poem 'Redcrosse': 'The way we exist/depends on him'. We perform the script, and the common script is what makes us intelligible and connected to one another. I am not persuaded by the exceptionalist tone of some Jungian talk about vocation, as though only a privileged few are called to the pilgrimage of the soul. Truth beckons all of us just as surely as deception tempts us all. This is why language, and indeed liturgy, matter so much, and why our national literary and liturgical heritage needs to be renewed and re-imagined; it signifies more than its purely aesthetic or antiquarian appeal. Spenser's famous (but often misquoted) question to Gabriel Harvey on the theme of barbarous prose, 'Why, a God's name, may not we, as else the Greeks, have the kingdom of our own language?' conveys his conviction (which Cranmer, of course, also understood well) that the vernacular can be shaped by literary innovation, and that with it, national culture can also be shaped.[13] As I understand it, something of this spirit also informs the *Redcrosse* liturgy, but in its conception, it implicitly rejects the belief that 'solidarity' in worship and spirit inheres in a single, canonical liturgical text. And yet, neither national solidarity nor authentic identity can be constructed out of nothing, without reference to context or historic roots. Williams writes:

> The struggle to preserve or revive national languages – Welsh, Hebrew, Basque – is not as comic or self-conscious as it may sometimes look. There is an important element of discovering what as a human *group* with a particular history you want to say. This also throws some light on our liturgical problems at the moment. We've lost a language which in its way was strong and flexible. We certainly haven't found a new one that is at all comparable, and so we don't know what we have to say in worship and retreat into inoffensive banality. Petitions about the Prayer Book seem really to be asking less for a particular book than for a language in which certain vital things can be said with confidence, honesty and imagination.[14]

For Rowan Williams, understanding of vocation – personal or collective – is what emerges when we discover what it is we want to say, when we find an authentic language in which to articulate our shared society and moral purpose. Liturgy potentially provides that script, which both transcends and earths the particular. Above all, it must manifest authenticity in worship and the reaching of heaven to earth as surely as the reaching of the soul to heaven, inviting us to 'shed the unreality [and banality] that suffocates the very life of the soul'.

In this year of remembering the three hundred and fiftieth anniversary of the 1662 Book of Common Prayer, the ambiguous legacy of the traditional English liturgy for national religious life needs to be held in view. It should not be forgotten, above all, that it was initially employed as an instrument of division and domination, prescribed in the Act of Uniformity, resulting in the expulsion of thousands of conscientious clergymen. For all the sublimity of

Cranmer's prose, the text in this form also represents the English church at its most security-conscious, propagandist and totalitarian. The Prayer Book will justly be celebrated widely in 2012, but its origins should remind us that liturgy *can be* used in oppressive ways, and that the idea of catholicity has its victims. In his infamous Preface to the Crockford's Clerical Directory in 1987, the church historian Gareth Bennett lamented the decline of the 'English style' in Anglicanism, exemplified by, among other things, the 'disappearance' of the Book of Common Prayer in favour of modern and plural forms of worship. The new liturgies, he wrote, were 'not so much a factor for unity as a sign of increasing diversity', at both an ecclesial and national level.[15] Bennett found himself in the tragically ironic position in which so many champions of catholicity in the Church of England have found themselves: that of opposition and dissent, themselves the focus of disunity. Under the pressure of media attention which broke his anonymity, this was existentially devastating, and Bennett's subsequent suicide stands as a testimony to the deeply felt historical and spiritual tensions at the heart of Anglican identity in the modern world. Seemingly doomed to a perpetual battle between traditionalist and modernizing impulses, England's church and its liturgical languages embody the paradoxes of a nation steeped in history, in religious and cultural continuity, but also conditioned by that very history, religion and literary culture to pioneer, explore and reform. We cannot escape the reality that one of the distinctive characteristics of English vernacularity and religion is the historic dialectic between tradition and renewal, between uniformity and diversity, between authority and dissent. These interplays have been creative as well as destructive: they can be again.

Few historians of English religion would be able to accept Bennett's version of catholic continuity, and it has been a dangerous myth. In particular, it has recently been argued that a distinctively 'Anglican method', rooted in scholarship of the early church Fathers, only flourished late in the church's formation as it defined itself in opposition to its two great enemies or demons: Roman Catholicism and, after the Civil Wars, radical Protestants.[16] Even then, there were two 'golden ages' to which Anglicans appealed: not only the earliest centuries in the life of the church, but also the early Reformation, when England's religious identity was fought out amid bitter controversy and political transformation. What characterized both periods was not harmonious uniformity but rather the contested and provisional character of the church and its worship. Indeed, one central liturgical emphasis of the English as well as the continental reformers, which few who love the term would regard as 'catholic' and which has been bemoaned by aesthetes and ecclesiastical historians, was their iconoclastic impulse. Iconoclasm marked deep discontinuity. Anything which threatened to take the place of God in worship – and of course there was widespread disagreement over what those things might be – should be removed as an idol. Lutherans and many later English Protestants preferred to focus on interior iconoclasm, purging the heart of its idols, and it seems to me that this view of iconoclasm is an essential dimension of the Christian quest for wisdom, which is in constant need of renewal. The slaying of the dragon may be seen in this light.

When we turn away from you towards false gods
Rescue us
When we fear that we have lost the fight
Renew our strength (Redcrosse)

All this is to suggest that experiments in liturgy such as *Redcrosse*, especially those which draw imaginatively on our ambiguous heritage expressly in order *not* to indoctrinate or exclude, may potentially be 'catholic' as well as distinctively 'English' in quite a different sense from the Prayer Book. What this poetic, oblique yet honest text does is to subvert the petrified *projections* of English and Anglican identity which are partial, clannish and illusory, the totalizing visions of church and nation which the eighteenth century Anglican mystic William Law complained about in his own age:

> Now this is the greatest evil that the division of the church has brought forth; it raises in every communion a selfish, partial orthodoxy, which consists in courageously defending all that it has, and condemning all that it has not. And thus every champion is trained up in defence of their *own truth*, their *own learning*, and their *own church*; and he has the most merit, the most honour, who likes everything, defends everything among themselves, and leaves nothing uncensured in those that are of a different communion. Now how can truth, and goodness, and union, and religion, be more struck at, than by such defenders of it?[17]

Whatever threatens the tyrannical unconscious, however – which is not to say the unconscious is always or only tyrannical – is bound to generate hostility. The Jungian writer Robert Moore describes a form of unconscious narcissism which infects groups and whole societies as well as individuals: 'a malignant, pathological tribalism that wreaks havoc on their neighbours and threatens the rest of the world'.[18] While the contemporary Church of England can hardly be accused of representing this 'malignant, pathological tribalism', it certainly contains defensive and tribal elements, and the vitriol stirred up by the Manchester event reflects the depth to which these currents run in English society more widely.

A thronging diamond mine

*Don't get lost in stories, if you want to get lost in a wood
and, at this juncture, you really do – with that look
of embowerment softening your eyes.*

JO SHAPCOTT

*And struggle will seem an ecstasy,
Failure a thronging diamond mine*

EWAN FERNIE

The novelist Edith Pargeter once wrote, 'it takes a lot to wound a man without illusions.'[19] The same, presumably, applies to a woman, and there have been times (still are) when it wouldn't take very much to wound me, badly. Spiritual warfare, as I have described it and as it is evoked in the liturgy, is the battle against illusions, fantasies and 'true-seeming lyes' (*FQ*, 1.1.38), which may be conceived as hypostatized evil, and the wounds which the Redcrosse knight bears at the outset of his quest as 'the symbol of our restlessness', are, I think, the signs of his vulnerability to hypocrisy and deception. I have been unable to disentangle my own struggle with unreality from the process of reflection: the imaginative rethinking of national identity, and the exploration of the allegorical deeps of *The Faerie Queene* and the poetry of *Redcrosse*. I have wanted to meditate briefly in this chapter on how the project has captured my own spiritual imagination.

During Lent 2009, around mid-March, I travelled up from Oxford to the Lake District for a retreat with a friend, at a rather difficult time when we were both engaged in some introspection, chiefly about personal vocation. One of my projects for the retreat was to spend time reading *The Faerie Queene*, but half-deliberately I failed to take my hefty Longman edition with me, following a rather feeble hunch that I would find a copy on the way. None of the various bookshops I had time to browse in Oxford had a copy; not a single book store in Windermere or Ambleside stocked the damn thing. Apparently there's not a thriving market for the Spenserian stanza in the Lakes. I'd given up and given myself over to pleasant walks and the Psalms, but it was in tiny Grasmere that I finally found it, after taking the meandering pathway from Rydal, a route traditionally used by coffin-bearers. Among the teashops and outdoor-clothing retailers, Sam Read's Bookshop is an absolute treasury: full of poetry, not just prolix Wordsworth, who is so intimately associated with the villages of Grasmere and Rydal. It is described in travel guides as 'the kind of place you'd expect to find a mysterious novel and tales of secret enchantment', and 'a truly magical place'. Indeed, there it was, my thick wedge of a Penguin classic, which I took with me down to the lake, looking for a place to sit and read. There by the water's edge was a lonely little ramshackle shed that served tea in tin pots and china cups, with a few outdoor benches and three colourful little rowing boats jostling against the mooring. The hanging sign by the roadside read 'FAERYLAND', and it was one of the most eerily beautiful places I have ever seen.

On that afternoon, I remember that the hills were engulfed in cloud. In the uncertainty of my situation at that time, I felt suddenly called to sit with the unclarity, and not to try to fight my way out of it with guessing. The book was – inarticulately, before I'd even started to read it – a companion in the unknowing, and it struck me as significant that in the letter of the author, Spenser defends his decision to 'expresse Holynes', 'clowdily enwrapped in Allegoricall devises'.[20] It also brought to mind Wordsworth's famous description of 'Sweet Spenser, moving through his clouded heaven'; and his tribute to Grasmere with its 'blended holiness of earth and sky/Something that makes this individual spot/This small abiding place of many men ... A whole without dependence or defect/ Made for itself and happy in itself/Perfect contentment, unity entire.'[21] Grasmere and its poetic heritage were sacred to me that day. The experience raised my hopes for the Redcrosse knight as a fellow pilgrim: I imagined I would be taken with him on a sort of mystical ascent towards the joyful clarity of fulfilled vocation. But, as I have mentioned, there were many things which troubled me in the allegory, and although there were many pleasures and surprises in the reading, I can't pretend to have found it especially edifying devotionally. The only moment which I found truly moving was the vision of Una as 'Forsaken Truth' seeking after her beloved in the wilderness, driven to madness by anguished bereavement and desire (1. Preface to Canto 3). (Later, I learned that Wordsworth would read the *Faerie Queene* in Dove Cottage at Grasmere with his wife, Mary Hutchinson, and that together they were affected by 'How Una, sad of soul, in sad attire,/The gentle Una, of celestial birth,/To seek her knight went wandering o'er the earth.')[22]

There are two journeys in this story: one of them belongs to the Red Crosse Knight, and the other belongs to Una, in her chasing after the one who had forsaken her. It's the success of *her* quest, and the crushing failure of *his*, which leads to the way of holiness. I was struck also by the voice of Una which, when Redcrosse is tempted to self-destruction, cries in furious reproach 'Why shouldst thou then despeire, that chosen art?' (1.9.53). In my groping after illumination and security, it had not occurred to me that I was straying away from truth, and that it was in pursuit of me: forsaken, seeking, longing, exiled. Truth was to be found in turning. I had spoken rather tentatively of the mystical 'clouded heaven' and the darkness of allegory in the first group consultation, and how that resonated with my personal experience of wrestling with uncertainty and opacity. However, in the authentic quest for truth, heaven breaks through the clouds, in revelation, in the 'sacramental word' which proclaims in the words of Andrew Shanks' 'Air: A Psalm of Many Voices':

'Let there be light!' till kingdom come, when all at last is lit.

At times, I was concerned that holiness was presented in the liturgy *only* in struggle and darkness, and that the light of heavenly truth remained effaced – 'the unknown God' who is 'beyond all winning and having'. And yet, restlessness was the necessary starting point.

In the allegory, darkness and despair are an essential part of the process by which regeneration comes: 'good grows of evils priefe' (1.8.43). Grace redeems the whole, even the waywardness and deception. The pursuit of holiness isn't what characterizes Redcrosse's quest throughout: he is proud, joyless and reckless at the outset, cruelly marked with deep ancient wounds, riding an angry, disdainful steed, and fit for knightly jousts and games, but not, perhaps, for the love of his fair Una (a personification of virgin truth, and the church as the apocalyptic bride). There is a moment of 'turning', of repentance and conversion at the House of Holiness and the heavenly city which seemed to me just as much a climax as the conquest of the dragon and the final nuptials. There *is* a shape to Redcrosse's journey, there is a point of illumination and apotheosis as St George. There is even a harrowing of hell, and a stark, unbearable exposure of all that had been false and decayed and tyrannized. It is evoked in the liturgy in the confession, and in the 'Psalm of Many Voices' where 'fresh oxygen (thank God) floods in':

'Breathe freely now!
The "God" you thought you knew – that wasn't *God.'*

Light and freedom are disclosed to the Redcrosse knight in the failure of his spiritual crusade, at the point at which his strength is ruined and he has been overcome and imprisoned by Duessa's lies and the giant's tyranny. Upon seeing 'all his vitall powres Decayd', Una laments 'That of your selfe ye berobbed arre' (1.8.41–2).

My story is marked by holiness only in the sense that it is for Redcrosse – it is at the point of crisis that truth, about God and oneself, breaks in through the clouded heaven. Discovering the call to be, 'when all the games have stopped', has for me taken the form of resisting two particular temptations to unreality, which are not uncommon in the academic profession. Both tend towards isolation from one's community and from God, and involve the creation of false enemies and a false self. The first and most obvious temptation is to illusions of grandiosity: the myth of one's own autonomy and capability in isolation from others. Such myths sustain a competitive rather than a collaborative environment, a false sense of entitlement, and lead to intellectual myopia, megalomaniac empire-building and personal and professional feuds. The other tendency, one which I have found especially seductive, is towards obscurity and withdrawal, into a life which is unchallenged and apparently secure. This, I have found, is just as destructive a temptation as the lure of grandiosity, its comforts just as superficial. Jung's devouring dragon is at work in both of these drifts from reality, annihilating that which is truly creative and beneficial to others in the human intellect and spirit. These false selves are, indeed, interdependent and part of the same oppressive deception. The grandiose self tyrannizes over perceived weaknesses and sees only threat rather than support and help in the strength of others; the diminished self is the tyrannized, the one punished for its weakness, which sees judgement and condemnation rather than encouragement in figures of authority. Only when these cursed conspirators had utterly sapped my confidence and threatened to extinguish my spirit did the turn away from isolation and from deception begin.

> *How to keep faith. Here in the field where the grass*
> *has recovered but we have forgotten its names,*

*and clouds that are carved in the shape of a cave
pour forth in torrents of melting silver the rain.*

ANDREW MOTION

It is easy to see how these temptations to unreality, to isolation, grandiosity and withdrawal, might affect us collectively as well as individually. What, then, is to be done to defeat the dragon, finally? It is not primarily in condemning or exposing those tendencies in individuals, except where such exposure becomes necessary to hold to the truth. The spiritual way can become a hideous masquerade where tyranny is replaced with tyranny, in the hypocritical guise of freedom and openness. What is needed is clearly real transformation, in the blazing lucidity of divine love. Is it possible that our emblem of English patriotism, the dragon-slaying warrior, might stand for something else after all, something that is growing among us as surely as cultural chauvinism or xenophobia? That is our coming to consciousness, our passionate desire to cast light into the places (both internal and external) of darkness, secrecy and fear – of corruption, unreality, abuse and injustice. I conclude with the Collect for St George's Day, which features in the liturgy, with my own prayer that, in these days of crisis, all spiritual tyrannies will be subjected to rigorous examination, for 'nothing is covered up that will not be uncovered, and nothing secret that will not become known' (Matthew 10.26).

*God of hosts,
Who so kindled the flame of love
In the heart of your servant George
that he bore witness to the risen Lord
by his life and by his death:
give us the same faith and power of love
that we who rejoice in his triumphs
may come to share with him*

the fullness of the resurrection ;
through Jesus Christ your Son our Lord,
who is alive and reigns with you,
in the unity of the Holy Spirit,
one God, now and for ever.

Notes

1 All Biblical references are to the AV.

2 References are to Edmund Spenser, *The Faerie Queene*, ed. A. C. Hamilton, 2nd edn. (New York and London: Longman, 2001).

3 See, for instance, Lyndal Roper, *Witch Craze. Terror and Fantasy in Baroque Germany* (London: Yale University Press, 2004); Deborah Willis, *Malevolent Nurture: Witch-Hunting and Maternal Power in Early Modern England* (Ithaca: Cornell University Press, 1995).

4 Several recent review articles attest to this shift: see, for instance, Alon Confino, Ute Frevert, Uffa Jensen and Lyndal Roper, 'Forum: History of Emotions' in *German History*, Vol. 28, No. 1 (2010), 67–80; Susan J. Matt, 'Current Emotion Research in History: Or, Doing History from the Inside Out', in *Emotion Review* Vol. 3, No. 1 (2011), 117–24.

5 Eusebius, *Historia Ecclesiastica*, Introduction to Book V, *Nicene and Post-Nicene Fathers*, ed. Philip Schaff (New York: Charles Scribner's Sons, 1904), Series II, Vol. I, p. 211.

6 Carl Gustav Jung, *Four Archetypes* (Abingdon, Oxon: Routledge, 2003), p. 15.

7 Jung, 'The relations between the ego and the unconscious' in *Two Essays on Analytical Psychology*, Collected Works of C. G. Jung, Vol. 7 (London: Routledge, 1966, 2nd edn.), para. 261, p. 170.

8 Jung, 'Definitions' in *Psychological Types*, Collected Works of C. G. Jung, Vol. 6 (Princeton, NJ: Princeton University Press, Bollingen Series XX, 1971), para. 758, p. 448; 'On the Nature of the Psyche', in *The Structure and Dynamics of the Psyche*, Collected Works of C. G. Jung, Vol. 8 (Princeton, NJ: Princeton University Press, Bollingen Series XX, 1969, 2nd edn.), para. 432, p. 226.

9 Jung, *The Psychology of Kundalini Yoga: Notes of the Seminar Given in 1932*

by C. G. Jung, ed. Sonu Shamdasani (Princeton, NJ: Princeton University Press, 1996), p. 40.

10 Marion Woodman, *The Ravaged Bridegroom: Masculinity in Women* (Toronto: Inner City Books, 1990), p. 18.

11 Rowan Williams, *A Ray of Darkness: Sermons and Reflections* (Cambridge: Cowley Publications, 1995), p. 152.

12 Ibid., p. 150.

13 See Richard Helgerson, *Forms of Nationhood: the Elizabethan Writing of England* (London: University of Chicago Press, 1992), pp. 25-40.

14 Williams, *Ray of Darkness*, p. 156.

15 Gareth Bennett, 'Preface to Crockford's Clerical Directory 1987/88', in *To the Church of England: Essays and Papers*, ed. Geoffrey Rowell (Worthing: Churchman, 1988).

16 Jean-Louis Quantin, *The Church of England and Christian Antiquity: the construction of a confessional identity in the seventeenth century* (Oxford: Oxford University Press, 2009).

17 William Law, in Christopher Walton ed., *Notes and Materials for an Adequate Biography of The Celebrated Divine and Theosopher, William Law* (London: printed for private circulation, 1854), p. 179.

18 Robert L. Moore, *Facing the Dragon: Confronting Spiritual and Personal Grandiosity* (Wilmette, IL: Chiron Publications, 2003), p. xxiii.

19 'Ellis Peters' aka Edith Pargeter, *The House of Green Turf* (London: Collins, 1969), p. 96.

20 Spenser, 'A Letter of the Authors expounding his *whole intention in the course of this worke*' to Sir Walter Raleigh, in Michael Payne and John Hunter (eds), *Renaissance Literature: An Anthology* (Oxford: Blackwell, 2003), p. 245.

21 William Wordsworth, 'The Prelude, Book III' and 'Home at Grasmere', in *William Wordsworth*, ed. Stephen Gill (Oxford: Oxford University Press, 2010), pp. 338, 192.

22 From Dedication to *The White Doe of Rylstone* (1815), cited in David Hopkins ed., *The Routledge Anthology of Poets on Poets: Poetic Responses to English Poetry from Chaucer to Yeats* (London: Routledge, 1990), pp. 91–2.

Redcrosse at Manchester Cathedral. By Tony Hardy

6

From Romance to Ritual: Redcrosse *and Spenser's* Faerie Queene

John Milbank

Introduction

Unlike the other contributors to this book, I was not involved in the devising of *Redcrosse*, nor was I an advisor for this process. However, I participated in the liturgy at Manchester, which I found to be a quite overwhelming experience. Since then I have read *The Fairie Queene*, and the other essays in this book. What follows is a reflection upon all this material.

Writing emergency

In the *Redcrosse* liturgy one moment of Elizabethan trauma has spoken to another. Today we face a crisis of Englishness and a not unrelated crisis of Anglicanism.

The English identity may have been the core of a British one, but it was also subsumed within it, sacrificially lost to the compass of its own ambitions, generously or haughtily reduced to a matter of language, style and political custom. With the formal loss of empire and unease about its continuing informal imperial role, belief in 'Britain' has begun to wane in the Celtic margins, leaving England with nowhere obvious to go. Meanwhile, the option of 'Europe' as a successor project for the European nation-states has become enfeebled both by lack of English enthusiasm and a failure of all European nations to agree upon its fundamental terms of operation.

Equally, the modern English nation, in its separation from Rome and partial turning from the Continent towards the high seas, had been inseparable from the Anglican Church settlement. But increasingly the Church of England finds itself unable to lay claim to any pivotal English role while an alternative future of Anglicanism as a post-imperial global communion does not look very viable in the face of intransigent cultural divisions and the absence of any habit of centralised global authority.

In the face of this double crisis, to turn for inspiration to Edmund Spenser's romance epic, *The Faerie Queene*, might seem bizarrely quixotic. For if this text has fallen so out of fashion, then is this not in part (besides its apparently didactic moralising) because it is the now embarrassing manifesto for an English imperial mission, based upon a near-idolatrous cult of monarchy, disdain for other cultures as supposedly 'barbaric', and a more or less paranoid identification of the Church of Rome with Antichrist and the scarlet woman? Are these not just the most ugly national traits of which we must now repent, albeit suspiciously late, given that apology for past vaunting is perhaps our only safe option in our current potentially parlous plight?

Of course there *is* another option, even if it is the path of pathetic and possibly dangerous folly: this is the path taken by the far-right and its imitators (some aspects of the *Daily Mail*, for example) of trying to invent pure ethnic and land-based 'Englishness' that never was, the post-imperial path of a nation deciding to turn in upon itself and define itself in terms of a crudely stockaded purism. Currently the Hungarians seem to be going in just this poisonous direction.

The devisors of the *Redcrosse* liturgy appear to have been motivated to some considerable degree by a desire to head off any such undesirable option. One might say that they have sought a homeopathic cure for an emerging disease: in order to combat poisonous patriotism and a sick cult of St George, they have decided to see if it is possible to embrace positively both saint and country. And the sense of homeopathy is much reinforced by the apparently perverse decision to embrace Spenser. Just how can his already contaminated St George help us to re-invent this figure in the present?

But this option has proved just as correct as it is bold. For if *The Faerie Queene* can be read retrospectively as a manifesto for Protestant imperial triumph, even so Spenser's 'Una' was scarcely Kipling's, since she was more a hope than a reality, and Spenser's romance can be read as a response to dire emergency, even as an act of poetic desperation, for all that it so successfully reaches for a new, assured idiom.

To understand this, we have to look at the complex implications of that ugly Protestant paranoia to which Spenser undoubtedly subscribed. According to this paranoia, Antichrist has been at work at the very heart of the Christian enterprise almost from the outset. But does this mean simply that one repudiates most of Christian history, looking to return to a lost purity of the origins? For many Protestants that may indeed have been the case, but it was surely not so for Spenser, nor for many of his English contemporaries.

Spenser clearly realises that such an act of repudiation would be impossible, since it would leave us with too little that we could regard as identifiably Christian. So it is not, for him, that the unambiguously good has been displaced by the unambiguously bad, but rather that the good and bad threads have been, since the very near outset, hopelessly intertangled. Thus, for example, he is able to recognise that Ireland, before Britain, was once the fount of the finest Christian learning of the time, and yet he still sees Patrick's mission as compromised by its 'papal' allegiance.[1] More decisively, Spenser's deliberate attempt to resurrect medieval chivalry in an archaising poetic idiom (making use of defunct vocabulary and ancient techniques of alliteration and assonance) has to be regarded as an attempt to recover a medieval Catholic lay piety from its supposedly corrupting associations with medieval celibacy and monasticism. Here it should be noted that Spenser rarely attacks any specifically Catholic doctrine (or supports any specifically Reformed one): what he appears to hold most against Rome, in a broad humanistic tradition, is its spirit of 'hypocrisy', which under cover of a claim to an excessively other-worldly piety in fact pursues to subtle excess the vainglory of this world. This twofold complaint is allegorised in the poem by the figures respectively of Archimago and the giant Orgoglio.[2]

What is more, the fact that the 'quest' of the Redcrosse knight who is St George is as much for 'holinesse' as it is to find and kill the dragon (the former being the precondition for the latter) suggests not just a story of 'becoming genuinely religious', but also of seeking out genuine religiosity, amidst the wavering uncertainties of this world, as figured by the 'wandering wood'. This suggestion is reinforced by the fact that there is more than a little indication of a religious 'third way' being sought in the first book of *The Fairie Queene* by its Platonically inclined author.[3] So while the role of redeeming grace is powerfully and dramatically stressed, this is never entirely at the expense of the need for human initiative and human works – a point made in poetic terms at the end of the eleventh Canto, where the perfect synergy of human and divine will is conveyed through the use of pronomical ambiguity:

> Then God she [Una] praysd, and thankt her faithfull knight,
> That had atchieude so great a conquest by his might. (1.11.55)

And it would seem crucial that the quest of the knight is not simply for salvation, but for sanctification, for *pietas* and *devotio* taken in the round. Indeed the 'House of Holinesse' which George eventually reaches is presented by Spenser as an unhypocritical monastery, guarded by a lady telling her rosary. Within this house, as John Ruskin noted, it is crucial that the knight undergo penitential exercises of a recognisably 'Catholic' kind, and also learn to practise the traditional seven acts of mercy, while combining such Catholic 'good works' with equally Catholic practices of contemplation.[4] It is, moreover, possible to read the episode of *Kirkrapine* as an attack on Protestant iconoclasm as well as upon the supposed monastic spoliation of the wealth of parish churches.[5]

From all this we can see that Spenser's unjustifiable paranoia about the Papacy nonetheless gave rise to a newly sophisticated awareness of how the best might often be tangled up with the worst. In Andrew Shanks' terms he had become, indeed, alert to the possibility of 'propagandistic' distortion, even if, as Shanks would of course agree, he failed to turn this suspicion fully upon his own side.[6] Nevertheless, his new awareness allows him to see history as a site of perpetual crisis in a new way. For up till very recently, in his Protestant account, Christianity has been shadowed and near strangled by an obscene double. It is of course this doubling which he endlessly allegorises in *The Fairie Queene*.[7] Not only are knights often drawn away from their true ladies by false ones, and vice versa, the consequence of this seduction is itself a 'doubling' of the personality, a failure to achieve integration as a consequence of the division of affection – either by the individual, or by the national personality across time, as so well conveyed by Andrew Motion in his lyric 'Redcrosse'.[8] Ultimately this seduction is a matter of being possessed by demonic powers, wielded here by Archimago.[9]

Divisive and deluded doubling is for Spenser always the result of false enchantment, and it is here that one can grasp part of the reason why the setting of the epic in 'fairielond' involves much more than an entertaining fictional device. For the effect of the paranoid reading of Catholic history is to suggest that what once appeared solid has now melted into the air: that the heart of the real itself has so far been demonically distorted in a fashion akin to that of diabolical magic. Given such an insight, then naturally our world starts to seem closer to the ambiguous realm of faerie than might have previously been imagined. Survival in such a world requires a continuous process of divinatory discernment of true from false appearances, of good from bad entrancements.

But the more positive aspects of fairyland can also be related to contemporary crisis. Exactly what *was* England, outside papal blessing? Exactly what now was the English church? The thing called the 'state' (ideologically neutral, mediating different viewpoints and safeguarding property through its monopoly of violence) had scarcely as yet been invented, much less the 'nation-state'. The only conceivable legitimacy remained that of 'Christendom', and it was to this mantle that England therefore had to lay claim as a lonely island empire.[10] But quite how this could be the case, or quite how the monarch was supposed newly to channel all sacred validity required to be newly imagined. This is just what Spenser is attempting to do in *The Faerie Queene*. Within that poem Gloriana, the Queen of Fairyland, can mirror Elizabeth precisely because the latter's realm, its extent and its legitimacy have become somewhat misty and fantastical.

These remarks about Spenser all tend to suggest that he has been well chosen by the devisors of *Redcrosse*. For in a national crisis he already posed an intense question about our national identity and did not assume any easy answer. For him, moreover, the answer was indissociable from the question as to where the true religion, the true church was to be found. And he approached this question in terms of a quest for true piety, including true worship – *true service* in every sense, whether of the romantic beloved or of God. This true worship reached its consummation in the Red Crosse knight's glimpse of the heavenly Jerusalem, whose community perpetually contemplates God in St John's *Apocalypse*.[11] Hence the idea of a 'questing liturgy', a liturgical promenade, would seem to be a wholly appropriate translation of *The Faerie Queene*. Equally appropriate would seem to be the idea of a 'quest for liturgy' itself, conjoined to an invocation of the unknown God, as in Andrew Shanks' air-theme, or 'Psalm for Many Voices'. Thus *Redcrosse* builds up to a final participatory liturgical act, when the congregation build the cross out of the red roses as an image of 'Jerusalem' to which England, also, belongs.

The picking out of themes from Spenser, within a short compass, is also judicious: the 'doubleness' of everything is underlined and our consequent loss of self-control.[12] Equally the focus on the symbolism of the four elements is well-considered and the way these are seen as the four corners of the cross. In the liturgy, as in the poem, they clearly stand for the material world itself, for the cosmic and the human body, but also for the combination of body with soul, since 'fire' is taken by Spenser to symbolise the spiritual element.[13] This can be a sacred fire or the fire of unruly passion, in which case it may also double up as the instrument of divine wrath. For these reasons the ambiguity of the dragon in the liturgy – as both good and bad passion, most subtly invoked by Ewan Fernie's Spenserian lyric 'Fire Sermon' – is justified, especially in view of the fact that Arthur (the real hero of *The Faerie Queene*) bears a dragon on his crest, since he is destined to inherit the title of 'Pendragon' from his father, Uther.[14]

As for the four elements in general, their ever-shifting effects and combinations are for Spenser the very essence of the 'mutabilitie' of the world, with which *The Faerie Queene* is centrally preoccupied.[15] In Dante's wood one may get lost, but in Spenser's wood (like that of Birnam) the trees seem lost themselves and appear to keep shifting their positions, suggesting that if humans cannot find their way it is because the world itself is radically unstable and unreliable, however tantalisingly and often treacherously beautiful it may appear. For this reason Tim Garland's jazz pastoral (sounding like a kind of 'Vaughan Williams Bebop') with its plangent, wavering, wandering, seeking, interruptive lines, perfectly conveys the ontological besides the axiological mood of 'The Legend of the Knight of the Red Crosse'.

It can therefore be argued that *Redcrosse* successfully achieves a liturgy of the crisis of English national identity and has chosen Spenser as its reference point well. But it still might be asked by some: Can this be a validly Christian exercise, or, if it is merely in part Christian, is it justified, either from a Christian or a non-Christian point of view? More specifically, one might wonder first, what the rationale is for a 'poetic liturgy', a liturgy deliberately dedicated to a legendary rather than a historical saint. Second, is it right to present a Christian liturgy focused upon nationhood and can one really invoke Spenser while jettisoning the unacceptable ethical and political baggage?

I believe that both questions can be answered in favour of *Redcrosse* and its remarkable and hopeful ambition. But in order to make these favourable answers, it is necessary to probe a bit deeper.

Allegory: Poetic and Christian

First one needs to ask, how would one justify the translation of a poetic allegory into the idiom of a Christian liturgy? And to answer this, one needs to ask in turn: just what *kind* of allegory is *The Faerie Queene?* In his *Convivio* Dante identified two kinds of allegory and his classification can (with reasonable plausibility) be taken as a representative one for medieval and Renaissance understanding as a whole.[16] First, there is 'the allegory of the poets', where the poet models a fiction – such as the struggle of a hero with a giant – in order secretly to convey a moral or a spiritual message: as in this case, it might be the need to overcome one's unruly passions. Secondly, there is 'the allegory of the theologians' in which (according to longstanding tradition) the literal sense is not a fiction, but the given reality of nature or sacred history. Here 'allegory' (as Dante later explicitly says in his *Letter to Can Grande*)[17] means whatever in either nature or history points forward to the Incarnation and the coming of the Church. But in theology there are two further 'spiritual senses' beyond the level of the literal: first there is the 'tropological' which is roughly like the poet's 'allegorical', since it concerns the application of scripture to our own moral and spiritual life. Secondly there is the 'anagogical' which concerns everything to do with the 'last things', whether the fate of the individual soul or the final fate of all Creation.

The crucial difference here of course is that theologians are interpreting a given text allegorically, whereas poets are making up new allegories, albeit with intended meanings. However, this distinction can still leave some lack of clarity as to how the *Christian* poet is situated in the matter of allegory. Indeed, it might seem that Dante himself is unclear, since different commentators have read his remarks on this question in very divergent ways. For some, Dante in the poems in the *Convivio* claims to be constructing poetic allegories, albeit as a Christian, but in the *Commedia*, going by his remarks to Can Grande, he (astonishingly) gives his work the status of holy writ and requires that it be read according to the fourfold method of exegesis. For others, however, the *Commedia* remains within the terms of poetic allegory because it is a fiction. This fundamental circumstance is not altered by the fact that the allegorical meanings invoked are Christian ones, and therefore do invoke, at a secondary level, the 'fourfold' range of implication.

The second view must be taken to be the most correct: heaven, hell and purgatory are for Dante real, but he does not expect us to believe that he has really been conducted on a tour through those realms by Virgil and Beatrice. However, it is not completely right, because, as Charles Singleton once pointed out, Dante *does* say that the *literal* meaning of the *Commedia* is the state of the souls in the next world.[18] Thus while the intellectual means deployed by Dante to invoke this Christian literal truth are fictional, he nevertheless seeks to place his work within an entirely scriptural orbit precisely because the allegory of his poetic fiction is so transparent – much more so, for example, than that of Spenser's figure of the lady Una, who stands for both truth and the Church. Hence the more serious 'spiritual' meanings of his work concern their allegorical reference to Christ, anagogical reference to our final destiny and tropological application to our lives in the present. (It should be mentioned here that ever since Origen theologians had recognised that the Bible itself sometimes uses poetic fictions or allegories, like the parables of Christ, in order to convey theologically 'literal' meanings of spiritual import.)

The example of Dante shows us that, in fact, Christian poets were situated somewhat *between* poetic and theological allegory. The paradigmatic 'poets' were pagans, inspired by the muses and capable only of a remote groping after theological truth. Christian poets also might write muse-inspired fictions, but obviously were not supposed to 'bracket-off' the things known through Christian revelation. Hence their fictions must, at their best, allegorically invoke just those revealed matters, as in the case of many medieval 'vision' poems.

Dante's claim with regard to the *Commedia* therefore places him at one extremely exalted end of a shared poetic spectrum. What is significant for our current purposes is that Spenser makes a similarly extreme claim, albeit in quite other terms. It is true that his work is far more palpably 'poetic allegory' than is Dante's. However, his contemporary Michael Drayton already noted that Spenser was the first to transpose the term 'legend' from saints' lives to romances: each book of *The Faerie Queene* being entitled 'The Legend of ... '.[19] 'Legend' meant 'especially worthy to be read' and thus Spenser is removing his romance into a spiritual domain of significance for human instruction in a way that can be seen as parallel to the transposition made by his Tuscan forebear. This is clearly related also to the theme of 'salvaging' the Middle Ages already invoked: the *real* monks can no longer teach us, but *fictional* lay heroes and heroines of the Middle Ages can do so in a new, unexpected fashion. Since reality has proved duplicitous, it is safer to flee to fairyland .... This is a third reason for the geographical setting of Spenser's romance. Medieval romances tended to take place on terrains bordered by the fairy-realm, but Spenser's is actually set within it, while many of the knights and ladies are themselves fairies.[20]

But if the use of the word 'legend' tends both to equate with and displace older spiritual narratives, Spenser also insinuated a kind of radical continuity between the first book of *The Faerie Queene* and the New Testament itself. When the Redcrosse Knight finally arrives in the House of Holinesse he encounters Fidelia, who bears a Eucharistic cup in one hand and in the other:

A book that was both signd and seald with blood,
Wherin dark things were writt, hard to be understood. (1.10.13)

No doubt this signifies at once the New Testament and the uncreated 'book of life' spoken of in the *Apocalypse*. Yet it is difficult not to think that this description fits suspiciously well the *Legend of the Knight of the Red Crosse* itself, especially as Spenser described his allegory as a 'darke conceit' in his letter to Raleigh (*FQ*, 'Letter to Raleigh'), and also because he calls attention to the need for what I will unfold here as a 'red hermeneutic' of inspired faith in order to read properly the enigmas of the Bible itself: Fidelia's 'sacred Booke' is 'with blood ywritt/That none could read, except she did them teach' (1.10.19).

If this is the case, then Spenser's book is seen by its author as subsumed into the most sacred text of all. Given its repeated preoccupation with eschatological themes, one might then venture that Spenser saw himself as called by God, in a period of dire uncertainty, to write a work of singularly new but authentic inspiration and guidance which would rekindle the genuine sense of the Scriptures.

This benign suspicion is confirmed by Spenser's endless play, throughout *The Faerie Queene*, but especially in its first book, on the word 'red' as both the colour of blood (and so of life) and the past participle 'read' (or other cognates) of the verb 'to read'. The most striking instance of this occurs in the description of the tree of life which saves St George after his second fall, when Spenser makes diversity of meaning stand in for diversity of sound in order to make a rhyme from what would otherwise be an identical repetition of the word 'redd':

> There grew a goodly tree him faire beside
> Loaden with fruit and apples rosy redd,
> As they in pure vermilion had beene edide,
> Whereof great virtues ouerall were redd. (1.11.46)

'Redd' in the second usage here means most probably 'told' or 'declared', though the sense of 'read' is not thereby lost. The first 'redd' denotes the full blush of life, yet the pun of 'dide' invokes the blood of Christ's suffering, just as its literal sense qualifies pure, untainted life (rosy red) as in fact the unadulterated work of divine art (dyed). With supreme subtlety Spenser thereby suggests that the contamination of life by its alternative opposites – death and artifice – is in fact the very guarantee of its non-contamination as both created, and redeemed through suffering. In the *Redcrosse* liturgy it is as if the red cross is composed of these two lines that are scored through life when in the hope of re-making the world the participants collectively shape the red symbol of death-in-life and so of life-in-death.

And in the case of Spenser himself, he would seem to have written a 'red book' (indeed a 'red fairy book' long before Andrew Lang) because he supposed that his imaginative invocation of other realms – of Eden, of Fairyland, of the Golden Age lingering in the realm of Pastoral, of the pagan heavens and the higher, Christian heavens – itself contributed to the possible recreation of fallen reality. By thematising blood, both as life and as death, he is able frequently to indicate that this 'red' blood is also the blood of reading, the cipher that unlocks the world's secrets. Hence at two points in the poem, at least, the cup of eucharistic blood and the book of the word of God are presented as conjoined.[21] Although the pairing explicitly privileges the word, the very conjoining can be seen as an allegory of allegory and an allegory of the necessity of allegory – in a way, that, once more, seems highly tangential to Reformed orthodoxy.[22] For the conjoining appears to say that there can be no meaning without embodiment, any more than vice versa – no 'read' of interpretation without the 'red' of life and death. It follows, therefore, that Spenser's allegories – his personifications, scene-settings and dramatic narratives – are no mere instrumentally convenient because diverting 'illustrations' to self-sufficient truths, but are essential *expansions* or 'dilations' (to use a Spenserian word) of meaning that as abstract would remain merely 'sketched out'.

The additional Spenserian double meaning of 'red' – within the realm of meaning itself – as both passively 'interpret' and actively 'proclaim' or even 'institute' would seem to clarify further Spenser's commitment to allegory. His red book attains near-parity with Scripture because he has so successfully 'told' the truth that the literal spiritual truths which he invokes (like Dante) can be subjected to a fully scriptural hermeneutic: thus his symbols speak quite often of Christ and his Church and of the final apocalypse, besides most evidently and proudly of how Christian gentlefolk are to live out their lives on earth.

In that case, one might ask, isn't basing a liturgy on *The Fairie Queene* to concur with Spenser's arrogance, which maybe is less justified than Dante's? I think not, because his justifiable pride can be seen paradoxically as a consequence of his honest humility. Here Shanks' category of 'shakenness' is entirely apposite.[23] Spenser was truly and manifestly shaken by the times in which he lived – and in such a fashion that caused him to have a newly intensified sense of fall and redemption as both repeated and provisional processes within the *saeculum*. In this respect once more his wholly (and in the end, reprehensibly) exaggerated sense of Popish corruption nevertheless opens up for him the possibility that even within the course of ecclesiastical history the disaster of 'fall' can be reiterated and intensified. And, if that is the case, then the nature of this 'second fall' (which is exactly how Spenser sees things in *The Faerie Queene*) must be, by definition, a certain radical occlusion of the truth of the gospel. So much is this so, he would seem to imply, that Christianity itself must now to some degree be re-imagined, even re-invented – precisely if it is to remain or to return to what it always was.

Thus Spenser undertakes his re-imagining in no spirit of vaunting Renaissance arrogance, but rather in terms of a hesitating searching, which, not by accident, achieved only one quarter of the intended Arthurian epic of which even the massive bulk of the completed cantos of *The Faerie Queene* is but a fragment.[24] Ewan Fernie is therefore exactly right to say that one has a sense of each verse in this work as looking for its plot rather than narrating something already known.[25] This sense is, I think, encouraged by the way in which each verse is almost a self-contained lyric, rendering the whole work an almost infinite series of miniatures, offering us obscure tapestry glimpses into another world that is rendered all the more real through this compositional strategy.

The view of the composers of *Redcrosse* – judging both by their work and their accounts of their labours – would seem, then, to be in authentic continuity with the Spenserian response to crisis. Whereas he sought to write a new romantic addendum to Holy Writ, they have sought to write a Christian liturgy that would reflect, critically, on the very nature of liturgy, given the way in which Christian liturgy has sometimes been used to justify or to gloss over so much that now seems to us horrendous (though that syntax is as deliberately qualified as any refusal of 'propaganda' would surely have to be). None of them are so crazy as to imagine that every liturgy should or could be like this, but they make a good case (both argumentatively and performatively) for saying that some liturgies now should be, if we are not to sink into a defeatist complacency.

Once more though, their approach to 're-imagining' liturgy is quite drastically homeopathic. Instead of steering as far away as possible from all nettle-beds of propaganda, they seize hold directly of the ur-plant itself by trying to construct a non-propagandistic liturgy around the theme of English nationhood. This procedure might seem the height of perversity until one reflects, with Shanks, that actually we never can be free of twisted motivations that worm their most insidious ways into our noblest expressions. Nor, as I think all the contributors also recognise, is it true, since we are finite, that we could ever praise the absolute without also praising that which is local and at hand – these things being all that is ever known to us. Since a St George's day liturgy focused on England is completely upfront about this, it is in Shanksian terms the most 'honest', and so the most ripe for a radically unpropagandistic treatment.

This point can be usefully connected with the liminal situation of Christian poets, as already mentioned. One might want to say that this situation is quite distinct from the unambivalent site of Christian preaching and worship. But surely both Dante and Spenser call such a distinction into theological question by elevating the poetic into the doctrinal, and thereby implying that doctrine – especially now, in times of respective crises – requires the aid of imaginative fictioning? (Spenser explicitly suggests that Mount Sinai, Mount Olivet and Mount Parnassus are one and the same summit.)[26] Not accidentally, both poets wrote in the name of a purportedly valid reform of spiritual by secular powers and were thereby committed to a thoroughly 'integrated' understanding of faith and reason, church and state, without, for all that, losing sight of the distance between the two different dimensions.

One can argue here that their fictional but ideal 'making' of virtues and vices and their ultimate fates hovers between the human political making of history on the one hand and the divinely given realm of creation and grace on the other. As such it is able to rebuke our ordinary human making in terms of divine law, but at the same time it insists on the role of imaginative making for our adequate vision of God who, after all, originally spoke to the prophets by renewing their outward and inner imaginative vision. In this way something more humanistically ambivalent has been introduced into the courts of the sacred, and yet the sense of the gulf between created and uncreated, fallen and redeemed is by no means weakened but rather intensified.

It is intensified because it is now seen (especially by Spenser) just how the unholy can simulate the holy, while inversely the aspiringly profane can sometimes come to the rescue of faith, just as Prince Arthur, who stands for secular Aristotelian magnanimity, has to come to the rescue of the knight of holiness.[27] Yet the integrated character of Spenser's vision here is shown in the fact that it is Una, or the true Church, who assigns Arthur to this rescue, while his association with secular generosity renders him an appropriate vehicle for truly divine grace, invoked when the princely 'child' speaks of the sheer gratuity of every genuine aid, at the end of the eighth Canto of Book Two.[28]

My argument, then, is that both Dante and Spenser in effect demand of theology that it admit its own necessary contamination by poetic liminality, including our perpetual suspension between the partial truth of the pagans and the ungraspable plenitude of divinely revealed understanding. By this I do *not* mean that theology today (as too many clergy and theologians now desire) should retreat to the realm of 'art', combining the false joys of an agnostic 'as if' treatment of finitude with the alibi of a sublimely unknown infinite. This rightly receives the scorn of atheists like Alain Badiou who claim the speculative knowledge of the infinite as indeterminate chaos.[29] Instead, I mean that if we now see, having passed through the fiery bath of scepticism ever since Hume, that the trust of reason in the ultimacy of reason, or in the infinite reality of truth, requires an act of faith, while still hoping that faith can understand itself as reasonable, then it is clear that a poetic speculation taken as mediating the participation of the finite in the infinite as beauty or 'glory' has to be the third term here, as it was already for the German and some of the English Romantics. Dante and Spenser implicitly anticipated this insight, just as they were among its ancestral inspirers.

Thus both the two poets, in highly different ways, returned the scriptural to the realm of the poetic, to the sphere of the provisionally constructed which only reinforces the caution of genuine piety. But in a sense the architects of *Redcrosse* have gone still further by staging an actively new poetic raid upon the religious, in seeking to construct a liminal, allegorical liturgy.

Would the justification for doing this be the need to realise, today, a 'Christian' liturgy that would also appeal to agnostics, to 'questers' and to people of other faiths? I don't myself feel that that notion would quite grasp what is going on here, because *all* true Christian liturgy does those things – this is exactly why atheists can be moved or troubled by Anglican evensong or an everyday Mass on the Continent. As Catherine Pickstock puts it (as cited by Shanks), every true liturgy (and she is only using the Roman rite as a good example) 'stutters' – with lots of repetitions, seemingly tedious returns to penitence etc. – because it is in a sense a liturgy about how there might be liturgy, a worshipping in order that we might come to the place of worship.[30] For just this reason, the idea of a 'quest-liturgy' is a superb example of a radical re-imagining of Christian practice that nonetheless only finds again in a new way what has always been the case.

Conversely, I don't think it's really the case that the Christian element has been minimised in *Redcrosse*. If there is only one scriptural reading (Ephesians 6.10-18), then that stands out all the more, because the theme of putting on Christian armour is naturally *the* theme of the entire piece; for clearly the George sought for is a Christian saint who was also a mythical knight. In the same way, the brief invocation of Christ, his death and resurrection stand out clearly as the fulcrum of the saint's inspiration. And the God properly invoked as unknown is the Christian God proclaimed as such by St Paul to the Athenians, since he is invoked in the liturgy as 'Our Father' in the Lord's Prayer, identified with the incarnate Son who died on the Cross and is also described as a God of peace who is an 'infinite harmony' compared with our fragmentariness (a description that could extend beyond the Christian but would not encompass all and every notion of divinity). It is clear then, that the liturgy has not escaped Christian specificity – but then its architects confessedly realise that an escape from specific tradition is impossible and perhaps undesirable, since any attempt so to do would surely be the greatest and most dangerous hubris of all. Thus if, as Shanks says, 'Whatever is of heaven flares and flutters:/Nothing is simple, nothing's ever fixed', the image deliberately undercuts itself by invoking the idea of a flag which always denotes a particular identity. The wager after all of *Redcrosse* is to purify the image of the English flag, on the supposition that if we cannot reconcile the particular to the universal, then our hopes for universal unity must remain disappointed.

But can one nevertheless simply take the Christian imagery of the liturgy as a useful metaphorics for the inward spiritual life of the individual? There is naturally nothing invalid in such an exercise and it is certainly part of what is suggested. But I do not think that everything is thereby captured. For one thing, the notion that only fictional image and narrative is of spiritual significance, whereas historicity is religiously irrelevant, is not so much a mark of enlightenment, as a remaining at the level of pagan, rather than Christian allegory. And just because I think that *Redcrosse* is so authentically Spenserian, I do not think that it remains at that level.

The idea that Christian allegory is an 'advance' on pagan, poetic allegory is not some sort of arbitrary subjective claim, but is rather quite objective and specific. For the point is that it is an advance in allegorical terms: that is, that Christian allegory is a more allegorical allegory. This is because the crucial mark of allegory, as we have known ever since Friedrich Schlegel (but have been reminded by Walter Benjamin and Paul de Man), is its invocation of the dimension of *time*.[31] One can offer as the simplest definition of allegory: 'extended metaphor'. Metaphor itself lurks behind every sign (signs being mostly dead metaphors) and therefore involves the substitution of one thing for another in the course of history. Since meaning is in this way always indirect, one metaphor or sign requires illumination by another, and it is this endless process which generates language.

In this sense, as J. G. Hamann and then Schlegel saw, language itself is an allegory: a chain of non-identical repetitions in signs that runs parallel to the chain of non-identical repetitions in endlessly mutable events.[32] Allegory as a specific figure of speech tries to refresh language, in the same way that metaphor does, but it seeks to isolate some particular phenomenon in terms of a consistent pattern of variations. Were Spenser's personifications to be just mechanical, then, for example, we would learn nothing new about holiness, nor about the affinities and disaffinities between different ethical qualities. And sometimes he presents us with a figure whose exact allegorical resonance is not specified or is complex. 'Una' herself is both 'truth' and 'church' (not *only* 'true church'), and this surprising juxtaposition poses almost endless questions to her stories.

Hence it is not at all the case (as Coleridge supposed, though he was not consistent and is contradicted in theory and in practice by several other romantic writers – Blake, for example, is manifestly allegorical)[33] that allegory precludes the sense of a symbolic 'participation' of an image in the truth which allows that the image is irreplaceable for our sense of the truth. It is rather that allegory permits narrative also to be seen in this way, while at the same time reminding us that no 'symbol' is really detached from the historical and human process of the discernment and invention of signs. Allegory is indeed 'conventional', but then so is metaphor. Yet in neither case is this ground for an atheist suspicion, as insinuated by de Man: for it remains possible, as, in the end for Schlegel (whose views evolved consistently towards Catholicism), that the entire human cultural process, in continuity with nature, participates in the infinite divine *Logos*.

But what is more, the 'conventional', instituted aspect of allegory does not simply line up, as de Man supposed, with its temporal aspect, its extendedness – as in the case of John Bunyan 'once' having invented the figure of Mr Worldly Wiseman in order to illustrate fairly straightforwardly a didactic, unchanging Christian point. It is, more usually, pagan poetic allegory, under Neoplatonic influence, which tends to be relatively more conventional and yet unaware of its inherent temporal genius. This is because it usually concerns the voyage of a soul through a fixed, preconceived metaphysical geography. (This geography was first of all read into Homer etc. by philosophers and then fictionally invoked by writers such as Apuleius in *The Golden Ass*).

By contrast, Christian allegory, as already described, is at once less conventional and more temporal, because it concerns the arrival of something new in time which fulfils, yet in a totally unexpected and surprising way, the original allegorical meaning of the literal level: whoever, for example, would have imagined that the great national political story of the parting of the waters of the Jordan was *really* about one obscure girl's pregnancy? Yet at the same time, Christian allegory is more conserving than is pagan allegory of the literal level: whereas once I know I have to subdue my passions, I can forget about the giant, the birth of Jesus from a virgin will *not* (on pain of subsiding into anti-Jewishness) let me forget about Israel and her heroic armies, because however much they point to their fulfilment in the Incarnation, the latter can only be understood *as* the fulfilment of their earlier work, as of so much else. And once the literal, base sense has been re-affirmed in this way, then one also tends to become more aware of how even moral exhortations rely upon their tropes: maybe, in order to understand fighting our passions, we need to return to the childish stories about giants after all. Spenser certainly seems to have thought so, and for this reason (rather like Origen) he parallels the three 'spiritual senses' of his hermeneutics, which do not flee from literal time, with three 'spiritual senses' that guard the castle of *Alma*, or the soul: these are true memory, present judgment and wise foresight (*FQ*, 2.9.49–57).

In this way, as so many of the romantics noted, Christianity has had a permanent and totally bizarre effect upon Western poetics: on the one hand, everything real of whatever kind is regarded as being of significance, as 'mattering'; on the other hand, everything is seen as more than itself, so that equally we now inhabit a world of shadows and night, compared to the selective and idealised clarity of pagan antiquity.[34] As Victor Hugo put it, the world of Christian romance contains fairies and sylphs far more mysteriously nebulous than any Greek gods, who tend to be but humans writ large, and equally monsters and gargoyles far more exultingly appalling than any classical menaces.[35] Equally, in a created universe all is cherished, as all is from God, yet because it is from God all is also mysteriously more than itself. In a fallen universe everything sublimely but fancifully 'arabesque' is mixed up with the disturbingly but fascinatingly 'grotesque'. As for humanity, when it is diversely allegorised into its bestial depths and angelic heights, it may have evaporated and yet its truth has been told.

Clearly Spenser, like Shakespeare, exemplifies this Christian 'romantic' aesthetic – the very term being coined from the example of the 'romance'.[36] The most crucial way in which he does so is shown in the *realism* of his allegory.[37] I do not mean by this merely that poetry and myth provide us with an indispensable means for opening up certain dimensions of the psychic that would otherwise remain hid from view. I mean, rather, that by personifying abstract psychic forces, he is indicating that these forces are in a manner indeed personal and that they exist outside us as much as within us. In psychoanalytic terms one could say that they are 'drives' – though the term was already used in the Romantic era by Novalis. If one is a materialist, like Freud, then it makes no sense to imagine that drives are primarily 'within us', while if one believes in the reality of soul or mind, then it makes only an unlikely Cartesian sense to imagine that the psychic itself occurs and abides exclusively 'within us'. On this sort of basis and in terms of the elusiveness of a 'united self' (more aspiration than given reality) Novalis – jumping right ahead of both Freud and Lacan – made a remarkable defence of the idea that we are 'possessed' either by the divine or the demonic, with positive possession by the former being defined by the circumstance that it allows us to also to remain at one with ourselves.[38]

This analysis seems highly in keeping with Spenser's humanistic Neoplatonism: if we do not 'participate upwards', through a good doubling that allows our integrity, then we 'participate downwards', as we are possessed by forces that are outside our control, since their enmity to our true integrity necessarily implies both their exteriority and their hostility, as also argued by the desert father and philosopher Evagrius Pontus.[39] (This is why Jung, who locates evil within, has to see it incoherently as somehow 'good' and needing to be 'integrated'.)

The same 'realism' arguably extends to Spenser's conception of 'fairyland' as a whole. His comparison of it to long-undiscovered Virginia and Peru[40] is not necessarily simply coy, because he is heir to a long tradition which regarded the imagination as attuned to 'daemonic' realms (as invoked by St Paul) hovering half way between the physical and the spiritual, just as the pure mind was held to be attuned to the realm of the angels.[41] In *The Faerie Queene* the pagan gods have been demoted to the level of daemonic powers whose height is only the topmost height of fairyland, but there is no reason to suppose that Spenser – any more than Milton after him – had ceased to believe in some sense in the objective spiritual reality of the forces which they represented. This belief concurs with his 'hylozoic' commitment to a pansychism which gives a realist bent to the allegorical personification of trees, hills, winds and waters.[42]

In *The Legend of the Knight of the Red Crosse*, this realism impinges in three significant respects. First, were it the case that characters in this story were only ciphers for ideas, then one would expect all interaction between moral imperatives or counter-imperatives to be externalised. But, to the contrary, when the Knight is tempted to suicide by *Despeyre* in Canto IX, this is presented as an internal possession, conveyed with poetic brilliance by the former's 'capture' of the Knight's speech in such a way that his argument against suicide veers with near-incoherence into an argument for it between stanzas 42 and 43.

The same excess of person over allegory is shown yet more strikingly when George has to be purged of his involvement with blood before he can be permitted to glimpse the heavenly Jerusalem.[43] What are we to make of this? Why should he need to atone for warfare if this was merely spiritual? Surely he does not need to repent for his slaying of vices? The issue can only be resolved in two ways and preferably both at once. Either there remains an inevitable but regrettable element of violence against persons in our 'opposition' to sin, or else there is in truth no real fighting of evil that never involves any physical violence. Both these perceptions are surely true, and both tend to suggest that allegorisation for Spenser, far from being a fancy way of presenting the ethical, is rather a kind of *re-materialisation* of the ethical, in line with a rather uncomfortable sort of realism. Thus, for example, he invokes the myth that the juice of grapes is the blood of the overthrown Titanic giants, conserved by an angry earth. This perturbingly suggests that the blood of the eucharist remains ambiguously the blood of a necessary but regrettable violent justice, to which God himself unjustly fell prey.[44]

The second instance of allegorical realism concerns once more the thematic of doubling. On the whole, as already indicated, this is to do with a realistic dualism of good versus evil, as with the reworked classical trope of the 'two gates' of dreaming, the horn and the ivory (but in Spenser ivory and silver), which represent respectively intrusive delusion and the infusion of divine vision.[45] And typically self-division is brought about by the former, however it may gain entry. However, there is also a good doubling as instanced by the endless pairing of virtues throughout the poem, symbolised by the cooperation of variously talented knights, by the sisters Belphoebe and Amoretta who represent two modes of chastity (virginity and marital fidelity),[46] as well as by the several erotic pairings of knight and lady. One could of course reduce these to a monistic and psychological theme: namely the importance of integrating various components within the self. Such a view might once more threaten to reduce allegorical art to an instrumentalist detour.

Yet this reading is rendered implausible precisely by the teasingly double meaning of Archimago seeing his guests 'divided into double parts' (1.2.8) after The Red Crosse Knight has abandoned Una, wrongly presuming her faithless. Such a convolution cannot possibly just mean 'separated', but rather pinpoints for once a central *crux* of the entire epic: namely that bad doubling proceeds from the loss of good doubling, or inner disintegration from the loss of social role and partnership. Spenser also lines up the need for interhuman confession with this *topos*: 'double griefs afflict concealing harts' like 'raging flames' one cannot extinguish (1.2.34). Without such social consolation and social completion, we are not for Spenser alone, but rather rent from our true selves by the force of 'the malign *genius*' who presides over the hothouse false abundance of 'the bower of blisse' where he produces the glittering works of *envy* (2.7.47–8).[47] Thus the false self that divides us when we refuse others will be the bitter sham intrusion of others into ourselves by force of our attempts to steal, by an impossible outshining, their integral characteristics. For Spenser this is, however, a real demonic possession, because the 'true self' is the benignly alien presence of the true divine 'genius', who presides with an additional duality over outgoing life and returning death in the place of the Platonic forms which is allegorised as 'the gardens of Adonis' (loc. cit. and 3.6.29–39). It is the warped form of the divine in the other that becomes the devilish in ourselves.

The irreducibility of the literal interpersonal level of Spenser's allegory is further indicated by the stanza where Una is said to be *impersonating herself*, which invokes a longstanding Indoeuropean narrative trope, and suggests that self-identity must necessarily take the 'doubling' detour of art, which involves the search for a true self-imaging; without this mirror we will have no possible glimpse of the original, since we cannot, as a subject, perfectly look back upon our own self as we can upon external objects and objectively-appearing persons.[48] In the build-up to her nuptials, some nymphs spy Una and

> Then on her head they sett a girlond green,
> And crowned her twixt earnest and twixt game;
> Who in her self-resemblance well-beseene,
> Did seeme such, as she was, a goodly maiden Queene. (1.12.8)[49]

As is characteristic for this trope, true identity is guaranteed by an identifying object – in this case, a garland – which is a work of human art. This fact of course permits of imposture – the false wearing of the garland – but by the same token imposture can be trumped by irony: the true wearer can pretend to wear what she wears truly and the teasing game of the gravity-defying dance is outplayed by a concealed gravity of fact. But in this case the nymphs would seem perhaps really to know what they are doing: hence the implication is that *all* 'crowning', or all self-identification, is a matter of art as well as nature and therefore occurs 'twixt earnest and twixt game'. It is at exactly this point that both pretence and 'reality' have jointly to yield before ritual or liturgy, which alone first 'fixes' meaning by isolating, repeating and so 'naming' an action, in a manner that renders it 'representative'. Here it can be seen that the (non-identical) repetition of the metaphor intrinsic to allegory cannot truly be sundered from the literal (but also non-identical) repetition of the event to which it always runs parallel and which provides its imagistic base. It is just in this respect that allegory has already covertly invoked liturgy, and would seem almost to call for a transition to ritual – just as the entirely masque-like character of *The Faerie Queene* seems an invitation for its transposition into opera.[50]

In the case of the good doubling of 'pretending to be oneself', social recognition is involved because one can only be identified by oneself, as by others, as the bearer of a symbol or a role or a name. So a gap is intruded between the flesh-and-blood Una and her allegorical identity as 'truth' or 'church', just at the point where this 'queenship' is, in narrative terms, socially conveyed, and is only conveyed correctly in terms of her unique, individual identity as worthy of her attributes, which is communicated to the reader by her bare name 'Una', plus the unique characterisation of her actions.

In this way the episode of the crowning of Una confirms that one cannot always reduce the dramatic, interpersonal action of *The Faerie Queene* to a cipher for intrapsychic processes. The poem does, indeed, move outwards towards a ritual accomplishment as well as inwards towards reflective appropriation. In this respect it tends to revolve in a dimension of Christian as well as poetic allegory, because spiritual fulfilment is now a matter of unexpected event, or repetition, as well as interior undoing of ethical forgetfulness, or 'recollection'.[51]

This is further shown by the fact that Una is 'church', a collective reality that has contingently arrived in time, as well as truth – though she cannot be the true, universal church if she neglects the wider-than-Christian reality of 'truth', as the *Redcrosse* liturgy so rightly insists, in keeping with Spenser's humanism. Yet nor is there truth for Spenser outside the communion of blood which is the church, since truth has had to be recovered through repair within fallen time. Thus the aid given by Una to the knight of holiness is not reducible to the need that faith has for both truth and reason (in order to discern false seemings, for example). It also concerns a 'showing' of the truth as the true church which can only be a contingent, intersubjective process – indeed, without this demonstration, faith is all too likely to be a blind 'faith in anything'.

Finally, and most decisively, Spenser's allegorical realism is shown by the way in which his narratives are after all 'about themselves', just as Una dances exactly her own part. Arthur's rescue of George *might* suggest simply the need that piety still has of secular magnanimity. But the fact that it is sponsored by Una as 'church', and so is a work of grace, means that one is returned to the fictively literal event as actually an allegory of itself. The story of rescue symbolises the reality of rescue. Moreover, the humanly narrative element is doubly validated insofar as Spenser's humanistically 'Catholic' theology of the virtues (which may well have helped to provoke disapproval in some quarters of Elizabeth's court) would seem always to imply that grace is mediated by charity and so by the interpersonal. After all, he claims – and with Biblical warrant – that the highest saving virtues are chastity as charity at the personal level (1 Cor 13.13), and 'courtesy', or a style perfectly integrating inward sincerity with outer 'art', at the social level (1 Peter 3.8).[52]

The same analysis applies to Spenser's treatment of the sacramental. The *Redcrosse* knight is only able to defeat the dragon because he partakes of the magical grace of a healing stream (as superbly re-imagined by Michael Symmons Roberts in his poem 'Water Song' in *Redcrosse*) and of the red fruit of the tree of life – after a 'second fall' which perhaps symbolises the fall of the Church in time. One can certainly read this in terms of a passage of Catholic sacramentality into a Protestant literary substitution.[53] Yet even in this respect, the ironic effect of this substitution in many English poets (including Donne, the initially Laudian Milton, Traherne and Shakespeare – whether or not he was an Anglican) is to cause a kind of outbreak of 'pan-sacramentality' or even *ultra-Catholicism,* in which the double opposition to both perceived Catholic selective fetishisation and Puritan refusal of the corporeal and imagistic results in a new sense that the 'increase' or 'dilation' of natural fertility, including sexual love, is not in competition, but rather in syncretic union with the lure of the transcendent. This union is symbolised for Spenser by the transcendent/immanent figure of *Natura* in the concluding two 'mutability cantos' of *The Faerie Queene.*

Yet even in the case of the traditional ecclesial sacraments, the doubling of the cures tells against any idea that they represent merely an internal, unmediated grace. Instead, the poetic logic here is entirely that they represent objective baptism and the objectively healing effect of the eucharist. This is confirmed by the symbolic doublings of the joint work of sacrament and word already mentioned, where the fact that the word of the poem is a *fiction* necessarily implies a bending back of the word, as allegory, towards the physically representative or sacramental. So while Arthur's gift to George of a phial of blood which heals wounds no doubt represents the old covenant, as compared with George's gift of a New Testament which cures souls, this by no means, as we have already seen, implies the inferiority of the first gift. For the book speaks of the 'saviours testament', written in letters of gold – a story then of blood, written in burnished blood, which is itself about real blood, which the New Testament itself declares always to have flowed in one current through Israel up till its fulfilment in Christ's passion.[54] By a highly subtle theological inversion, Spenser's invocation of the grace of the new covenant itself gives a new pride of place to the physicality and historicity of the old covenant, and by the same token to the pagan classical roles of reason and nature.[55] Thus it is Arthur, the future idealised secular ruler, who is here the agent of grace, just as for Spenser it is Elizabeth who has saved true religion through the exercise of political might and wisdom.

It is also worth pointing out that, whereas Fidelia in the 'house of holinesse' holds the New Testament in her left hand, she holds the cup of the eucharist in her right. Indeed, one could argue that the house is in one aspect the grail castle and that George has been assimilated to the grail knight. This is indicated by the fact that Spenser tells Raleigh that in the so far unwritten framing narrative which precedes the action of Book I, George first appears at the court of the Faerie Queene as 'a tall clownishe younge man', exactly as Percival in medieval romances appears intitially at Arthur's court as a youthful holy fool, before winning for himself a suit of *red* armour from which he can from thenceforward scarcely be parted.[56]

For all these reasons we can therefore see that Spenser strives to blend a poetic, fictional allegory with a Christian allegory of the event as fulfilment that tends, in consequence, to exalt an earlier level of literal eventfulness. Above all, the final level of the literal (the level to which even the Bible must perforce at first refer) is that of nature, of the elemental, as *Redcrosse* so well divines. Is this level, the raw material of allegory, finally to be undone by allegory? Is the wandering wood merely an allegory of undesirable lostness, destined to be allegorised away by other allegorical terms of stability which automatically de-allegorise towards spiritual stasis? This question would appear to be posed by Jo Shapcott's *Redcrosse* poem 'What the Forest Said', where it is suggested that actually we *wish* to be lost in the entanglements of nature, beyond the clarity of plots (never thick enough) and that it is this natural tangle that enshrines the bower of restful bliss which we seek, which otherwise would be inaccessible by any normal, well-trodden paths. All the poet can do is construct an artificial maze by 'stitching trees together in a tale', but the trees themselves always trump this, by threading round us instead, as Spenser indicates by often punningly abbreviating 'pursue' to 'sew'.[57]

Shapcott's lyric insight is profoundly true to the spirit of Spenser. For the entirety of *The Faerie Queene* keeps offering us false or imperfect bowers and concludes with a philosophical discussion in which the very preferability of stability over change is put into question. The supremely false bower is the 'bower of blisse' which is characterised by a kind of surreality in which nature achieves the alien perfection of art, while art so conceals its artifice that it appears to be at one with nature.[58] In this coincidental stasis, the quester has been immanently removed from time – there is no growth or oscillation because blossom and fruit occur at once, nor is there any further need for creativity in the face of a stifling perfection.

Spenser's point here is surely that while nature requires the perfecting touch of art, the latter can still never quite match nature's continued beginnings and can only restlessly anticipate the re-perfecting of nature by the divine art at the eschaton. Thus we need to sustain the interval between nature and art if we are to preserve both natural vitality and human inventiveness. In either case 'alteration' is not entirely a bad thing, even though it ceaselessly kills life and destroys the good.

The 'bower of blisse' in the poem has taken over some of the attributes of an excessive, diseased and doomed fertility that belonged in Plato to 'the gardens of Adonis'.[59] But in Spenser, the latter, as already mentioned, is rather the figure for a kind of heavenly nursery, containing the seeds or types of all things that are to come, including souls, and to which all things return after death to be revived.[60] Already here, there is the suggestion that the contrast between change and stasis can be mediated by the idea of a circle.

But at the same time, this seemingly exhaustive round of birth and death is somewhat disturbed by Spenser's description of the genealogy of the fairies, who are the result of a Titanic interruption: Prometheus shaped a male called 'Elfe' from a mixture of different animals, and mated him with an angel or pure spirit which he found in the Gardens of Adonis and dubbed 'Fay' (2.10.70–1). Fairies, therefore, to whose race by poetic conceit the Virgin Queen is said to belong (she is no mere human then!) are a blend of the ethereally heavenly and the sheerly animal: they are 'daemonically' both more and less than the human, but above all this blend is mediated by human imaginative and ingenious art, rivalling the power of Jove – though not that of Jehovah. Within the natural 'cycle' there consequently resides the disturbingly interruptive presence of human fictional making, which artificially stays and yet thereby *augments* natural mutability by ceaselessly adding historical changes not obviously recuperated by the metaphysical composting of Adonis's nursery.

After the bower and the gardens, the next ideal landscape invoked by Spenser is the realm of pastoral in Book VI, within which is situated the dance of the graces, who are devoted to Venus. To their traditional number of three has been added Gloriana, the Fairy Queen, as a mark of the new communion of human imagination with the pagan heights.[61] Yet just because these are not the final heights, the knight Calidore must finally leave behind even this immanent stability in order to resume his quest in time to slay the blatant beast which, significantly, *he is unable to complete*.[62]

All the same, the dance of the graces is for Spenser a pagan prefiguration of the Christian resolution. This is above all because their dance is a *spiral* and not simply a circle. Following Renaissance convention (as shown, on one interpretation, in Botticelli's *Primavera*), the description seems to suggest that two of the three graces steps towards us, while the other one steps away from us.[63] This is to signify that, in the rhythm of gift-exchange, more must always be given back then has been received if the bond of charity is to be sustained, and a benign indebtednesss remain as the crucial social glue. Reciprocity here, is therefore *asymmetrical*, in such a fashion that a spatial circle spins off into a dance through time: a dance, that, in order to remain both circular and asymmetrical, must necessarily take the mode of a non-identical repetition.

This idea proves crucial for Spenser, when, at the very end of the whole poem, he reinvokes an apocalyptic scenario. For now it turns out that only the pagan height involves an absolute contrast of stability with alteration. For above this height resides the Creator God who is himself the author of change. Thus with artistic reserve Spenser invokes Christ only twice in the final book of *The Faerie Queene*, yet does so decisively: once, by speaking of his December incarnation in a parade of the months, and earlier by comparing the theophany of *Natura* to Christ's transfiguration.[64] *Natura* in this book stands 'beyond' the contrast between heavenly Jove and material mutability and can validly be compared to the figure of wisdom in the Bible – at once uncreated and created. The comparison with Christ suggests that, just as the truly transcendent unchanging God can join to himself time and change, so the real heart of reality is a kind of synthesis of identity and transformation.

Right at the end of the poem this synthesis is named as 'dilation'. All things

... by their change their being do dilate:
And turning to themselues at length again,
Doe worke their owne perfection so by fate. (7.7.58)

This is extracted from the penultimate verse of the seventh book. The synthesis of stability and change resides in the fact that, in a law-governed and *created* cosmos, things genuinely alter by becoming *more themselves*, through non-identical repetition.

But a final paradox is reserved for the final verse: the process of change cannot itself be immune to change and will in the end be changed into changelessness.[65] However, Christian apocalypse is not identical to Platonic eternity: for into heaven is finally assumed the perfect concluding of all 'dilation', all non-identical repetition, all the 'fairy' process of imaginative and historical invention. In this way, even at the vertical end, the value of an 'outwards' horizontal expansion of creatures further into their own natures is not cancelled or denied.

For Spenser this dilating growth occurs either by literal nature or by allegorical *poesis*, but it occurs most fundamentally in the interplay between the two, since this mediates the re-creative working of divine grace. A magical 'fairy' integration of nature and art must be sought, if the world is to be progressively redeemed, but at the same time a gap between the two must be held open, along with a distinction between the human and the preternatural or the 'fairy'. This gap constitutes an eschatological reserve that continues to anticipate the final advent of the angelic and the genuinely divine.

The suspicion of slander

All the above considerations tend to show why a 'poetic liturgy' based upon Spenser's 'poetic theology' could be a legitimate Christian response to our current late-Elizabethan crisis. Yet an unease about the political angle might remain. Is this an act of 'civil religion' in the sense of a sacral celebration of Englishness in excess of the specifically Christian? I did not myself experience the liturgy in this way, any more than I found its critical reflexivity to be exclusive of a popular universal appeal to all Christians and beyond.

For me the liturgy was rather a chastening reminder that we can never seek to be 'Christians as such' but only Christians in a particular time and place, as a particular people, involved in specific social, linguistic and political arrangements. The way authentically to represent the universal is in a specific, unique manner: thus another great poet of the patriotic, Fernando Pessoa, in his *Mensagem*, asked:

> What lies in the undersea abyss, struggling to arise?
> We, Portugal, the latency of being.[66]

The claim is not presumptive, because if we have faith in providence, then every strong, outreaching cultural identity must, if it is true to itself, be disclosive of the ultimate and most general. In this sense it must have a mission.

The *Redcrosse* liturgy implies that England's real identity lies in its mission to follow in the way of the cross and the quest for true holiness. That must involve, as it says, a continued and sincere repentance for all the English have done wrong and will continue to do wrong. But does that mean simply a foreswearing of the unacceptably 'imperial' aspect of Spenser's legacy? I would suggest that things are slightly more complicated than that. For *The Faerie Queene* itself remarkably anticipates and forestalls any easy accusations and recriminations. In many ways it is a poem on the side of life versus death and a poem prepared to embrace death that is part of life for the sake of more life – finally for the sake of eternal life. But paired with natural death throughout is the culturally negative force of slander and envy as symbolised by the 'blatant beast'.[67] In an almost Nietzschean, or better Blakean[68] (since Christian) fashion, Spenser claims to be restoring an ancient positive virtue of creative, this-worldly equitable acts, over against a legalistic mode of morality that would seek mainly to minimise danger and to censure inevitable mistakes and fallings-short.[69] Indeed, nothing appears more relevant today in his work than his denunciation of a culture which seeks endlessly to bring low the good and the noble, to such an extent that public figures become in the end so petrified that they are unable to take crucial decisive action.

Spenser himself felt that he had been slandered. But for what? By Lord Burleigh, it would seem for his original erotic conclusion to book 3 – where the gender-bending female knight Britomart, who is the synthesising type of chastity, consummates her union with Artegall (justice) seemingly without benefit of clergy – and more generally for his fawning cult of Elizabeth that went so far as to overturn all tradition by associating the masculine principle with the eternal mutability of matter and the feminine with a ruling, shaping power of formation.[70] (One can see how Elizabeth's closest advisor could have felt emasculated by a mere poet.) But while we might today be inclined to salute these refreshing attitudes to sex and gender, the 'envious' slanders of Spenser's romantic theology and cult of the feminine are indissociable from the slanders (as Spenser saw them) of Lord Grey's brutally bloody campaign in Ireland on the Queen's behalf and Spenser's part in it.

To this 'slander' then as now, Spenser would seem to say, in advance, 'you were not there; you have no idea'. Indeed to read his *Veue of the Present State of Ireland* is to realise both that he has, to some extent, indeed been slandered, and also that then as now the problem is that some English ill deeds proceed all too readily from their good intentions.

For Spenser does not speak such obviously disparaging nonsense about Ireland as we have often been led to suppose, and as Irish scholars themselves now increasingly recognise.[71] Thus he regarded it as originally more civilised and Christian than Britain, traced its people to the 'noble' Gauls and Scythians,[72] learned something from its folklore (while deploring Bardic glorification of violence, as he saw it) and much from its wildly beautiful landscape – *his* healing waters are those of Ireland as well as of England![73] If he nonetheless diagnosed in Ireland a unique tribalist anarchy, then this was not altogether wrong, given the unusually long-lived absence of an effective high kingship (unlike Scotland), while Spenser insisted that the Anglo-Irish had compounded a bad situation. And though he can be condemned for not fully appreciating the workings of *Brehon* law, would he not rightly accuse us of hypocrisy if we claimed not to share his anxiety that mere material compensation to relatives of the victim as punishment for murder and the periodic resumption of private property upon the death of the tributary owner by collective powers were open to abuse, and provided insufficient security for lives and possessions – especially, as he says, for those of the common people? As to the claim that he wished to use starvation as an instrument of war, this has to be understood as his counter-strategy for dealing with the chieftain class alone – who themselves, Spenser claims, were horrifically prepared to abandon the non-fighting members of their own people to hunger and the attentions of the enemy.

None of this of course justifies Spenser's conclusions that barbaric means of discipline must be used against 'barbaric peoples', including the suspension of trial by jury, however much he might have validly feared that Irish juries were especially liable to be rigged. But if he is guilty here, as he surely is, then this is not clearly a guilt that the English have outgrown.

Moreover, *The Legend of the Knight of the Red Crosse* would itself seem to reveal a certain half-repentant hesitation on Spenser's behalf. When Una or truth becomes separated from the knight of holiness, she falls prey to lawlessness, because reason without faith will start to act merely on behalf of selfish interests.[74] She is rescued by the playful satyrs, who represent, as Ruskin suggested, the natural inclination of nature towards virtue, even when human faith and reason have broken down. They correspond to a 'barbaric' grasp of culture (reminiscent of Vico's understanding of 'poetic ages'), to balance the ferocious destruction of the lawless powers by Una's lion which is a parable of the need for rough justice in 'barbaric' Ireland, as with the deployment of 'iron man' *Talus* by Artegall as Justice in Book V. Yet if the oblique encouragement to Elizabeth's own desire to supplement Grey's iron justice with a gentler 'satyric' equity exhibits a certain guilty reservation in that book, then still more is this indicated by the fact, also noted by Ruskin, that Una is assisted by extreme, untrammelled violence only when separated from her champion, who represents true religious faith. So the implication would seem to be, as Ruskin suggested, that it is *pure reason* (or alternatively a wooden ecclesiastical dogmatism, unsuffused by any spirituality) that is excessively hard upon false religion or 'superstition'.

In these ways it appears unfair to regard Spenser simply as the representative of a rightly abandoned imperial past. For, to the contrary, his guilt is rather all too much in continuity with our still in reality imperial present. But at the same time, Spenser's own reserves and yet his own reminders – in the face of reactive slander which tends to be an enemy of life and its exigencies – of the ethical impulses that can lead to international involvement, suggest that England (like indeed Portugal, or Spain or France or Scandinavia) cannot simply abandon her maritime and imperial legacy without a retreat from her human solidarity (which sometimes *does* require one spontaneously to take command, in fulfilment of equity, beyond the law)[75] and the spirit of 'dilation' or of horizontal 'expansion of the heart' which the reality of the Incarnation would imply is the only true way for the heart to be vertically elevated.

It follows that the invocation of Spenser in *Redcrosse* cannot possibly be compatible with an England conveniently resigned to 'being on her own', an England without Britain, without the Commonwealth or without the European Union (being 'with' these respective entities need not be alternatives).[76] For if Britain is (despite her condemnable degree of persisting if diminishing racism) a perhaps uniquely non-ethnic polity, a polity in which indeed George may well be black and all the more English for all that, then that is precisely because (as earlier intimated) it is *not* a nation-state: not a formally self-governing sovereign body positively united by a single ethnicity.[77] Instead it is one part of the United Kingdom – a monarchic and consensual empire, governing itself under the assumed grace of God. Just because this empire has no fixed bounds or definitions of eligible citizens, it is particularly hospitable (in principle, and to a degree in practice) to all sorts and conditions of human persons.

Therefore we should see it as finally more of a radical rather than regressive circumstance that Spenser re-imagined England and English Christianity in Ireland, and that he regarded his monarch as being of fairy rather than human stock in part because she was of north Welsh, Celtic ancestry. And we should not see it as regressive that the poem embeds the tale of the archetypal English hero in that of the archetypal British one, Arthur, whom the unwritten cantos would have linked with a European as well as Irish destiny.[78]

Let us not then in future, as English people, be in any way tempted to narrow our hearts and our natural human sympathies, whether intellectual, romantic, religious or political, in the name of an excessively fault-finding and self-upbraiding probity which hypocritically over-repents of a past which we can never fully understand and which we cannot now return to, even should we wish it.

For nothing could surely be further from the spirit of Spenser as invoked by *Redcrosse*, and his ceaseless hunting down of that purely destructive spirit of detraction, the blatant beast.

Notes

1 See Spenser, *The Fairie Queene* ed. A. C. Hamilton (London: Longman, 2007), 7.6.38. All references are to this edition. Also see *A Veue of the Present State of Ireland,* Renascence Editions, on the web at www.

luminarum.org/renascence-editions/veue/.html, last consulted 12 January 2012. In my considerations of Spenser's romance epic I am indebted to discussions with Catherine Pickstock who is planning in the long term a book-length treatment of Spenser's theology.

2 See *The Fairie Queene*, 1.1–2 for Archimago; 1.7 for Orgoglio.

3 Not only can one place Spenser in a Renaissance tradition of religious humanism, one can also see him as developing a lay poetic and chivalric theology, already extant in the Middle Ages. This whole topic remains under-researched.

4 See *FQ*, 1.10.124-36; John Ruskin, 'Theology of Spenser', Appendix 2 to *The Stones of Venice*, Vol. 3, *The Fall* (London: George Allen, 1906), pp. 217–20.

5 *FQ*, 1.3.17–18 and see footnote to stanza 17, p. 57.

6 See Andrew Shanks' essay, 'A Desire for the Impossible' in this volume.

7 I am very much indebted to my wife Alison Milbank for insights with respect to Protestantism and 'the double'.

8 '....... I see that he has taken to losing himself in the forest/one minute, and making his living there robbing the rich, //and the next has abandoned all this for a spell in the city/where hammers have beaten his kindness into new shapes.' And see *FQ*, 1.2.37.

9 *FQ*, 1.2.9. The bad doubling is also allegorically exteriorised in terms of the birth of monstrous twins as the result of Titanic incest at 3.7.47.

10 See Carl Schmitt, *Hamlet or Hecuba: the Intrusion of Time into the Play*, trans. David Pan and Jennifer Rust (New York: Telos, 2009).

11 *FQ*, 1.10.56-7. I am indebted to discussions with my daughter, Arabella Milbank, concerning literary uses of apocalyptic.

12 In the poem this doubleness extends (at minimum) to a duality of life, of death, of dreams, of healing and of inspiration. In the liturgy this is directly invoked in Andrew Shanks' 'A Psalm of many voices': 'For everything's double:/cry the canny clouds on high.'

13 *FQ*, 1.11.21. The duality of purgative and inspiring fire which turns to light is a crucial part of Christian imagery which can be traced back to Origen and of course to the Bible itself.

14 *FQ*, 1.7.31; 2.10.68.

15 This is one reason for the pivotal place of the invoked mythical marriage of Peleus and Thetis in the entire epic – this marriage being the occasion in classical tradition both for the heavenly pre-instigation of the Trojan war and for Jove's conception of the three graces (again crucial for the poem) on

From Romance to Ritual: Redcrosse *and Spenser's* Faerie Queene 173

his journey home from the nuptials. For Thetis was a shape-shifting nereid who could become flame, water, lioness, serpent … . To guard against the prophesied power of her potentially Titanic offspring Jove concurs in the marriage of this spirit of change to a human man, Peleus. For Spenser this represents the marriage of nature to art and yet the binding by art of nature.

16 Dante, *Convivio* (*The Banquet*), trans. Richard H. Lansing (London: Taylor and Francis, 1990).

17 Dante, 'Letter to Can Grande', in *Literary Criticism of Dante Alighieri,* trans. Robert S. Haller (Lincoln, NE: University of Nebraska Press, 1973), p. 99.

18 Charles S. Singleton, 'Dante's Allegory' in *Speculum*, Vol. 25, No. 1 (Jan 1956), 78-86. For the opposing view to that of Singleton see Richard Hamilton Green, 'Dante's "Allegory of Poets" and the Medieval Theory of Poetic Fiction' in *Comparative Literature* (1957), 118–28.

19 *FQ*, 1. *Proem,* see footnote.

20 George, Arthur and Artegall turn out to be changelings, humans swapped for fairy children. But Sir Guyon and other knights are truly elves. Spenser in fact re-accentuates the original proximity of the Arthurian stories to the realm of the *sidhe.*

21 *FQ,* 1.9.19 and 11.46–8. In the case both of the gifts exchanged between Arthur and George and of the two natural salves for the fallen George, it is clear that the eucharist is seen as healing the body and the Scriptures the soul, and that the first is relatively more in continuity with the Old Covenant. Yet this is not manifestly 'Protestant': the same bias can be found back in Origen and in Erasmian theology. The pairing suggest that the two must go together, while the physical healing effected by the eucharist has a bearing on supernatural destiny that distinguishes it from the pagan healing of Aesculapius, to whom Duessa turns to heal her champion at 1.5.39–41. One can also note here that, since the appeal back to the Fathers began already in humanism, it may be fashionably excessive to think that this characteristic of Anglicanism commences only after 1662. To the contrary, Spenser's writings, like those of Hooker slightly later, can be read as an already distinctively 'Anglican' attempt to appropriate in a new way both the Patristic and the High Medieval legacy.

22 By and large the Reformers were suspicious of allegorical exegesis, even though it was first exemplified by St Paul who indicated how it was crucial to preserving the unity of the testaments. Bunyan's *Pilgrim's Progress* is more a poetic allegorisation of the Christian life than a blending of poetic with theological allegory, as authentically achieved by Spenser.

23 Shanks, 'A Desire for the Impossible'.

24 Nevertheless, the *FQ* as it stands has arguably been given a deliberate provisional unity by its author. For it has seven complete books, representing perhaps the seven days of creation and a two-verse fragment of a further Canto of the final book, 'unperfite', in which the poet prays that he may see the God of hosts ('Sabbaoth') on the eighth day ('Sabbaoth'): 8.1–2.

25 Ewan Fernie, 'Through the Red Cross' in the present volume.

26 *FQ*, 1.10.54.

27 *FQ*, 1.8.

28 *FQ*, 2.8.56.

29 See Alain Badiou, *Briefings on Existence*, trans. N. Maradrasz (New York: SUNY University Press, 2006), p. 29.

30 Catherine Pickstock, *After Writing: On the Liturgical Consummation of Philosophy* (Oxford: Blackwell, 1998).

31 Friedrich Schlegel, *Philosophical Fragments*, trans. Peter Firchow (Minneapolis: Minnesota University Press, 1991); Paul De Man, 'The Rhetoric of Temporality', in *Blindness and Insight* (London: Routledge, 1983), pp. 187–228; Walter Benjamin, *The Origin of German Tragic Drama* (London: Verso, 2011).

32 See De Man, 'The Rhetoric of Temporality', p. 189.

33 See De Man, 'The Rhetoric of Temporality', pp. 191–3.

34 See, for example, Jean Paul Friedrich Richter, 'School for Aesthetics', in Novalis et al., *German Romantic Criticism*, ed. A. Leslie Willson (New York: Continuum, 1982), pp. 54–5.

35 Victor Hugo, *Préface de Cromwell* (Paris: Larousse, 2009).

36 The British romantics were enthusiastic readers of Spenser, while the German and French romantics tended to regard Shakespeare – even more than Dante and Milton, whom they both appreciated – as *the* Christian poet, and for that reason the exemplary 'romantic' writer.

37 Recent scholarship has conclusively shown that romanticism was philosophcially defined by its commitment to *realism* and a realist theory of the imagination – as unable to construct either the self or nature, but as ironically our only and necessarily constructive mode of access to them –*in opposition* to idealism. See, crucially, Manfred Frank, *The Philosophical Foundations of Early German Romanticism*, trans. Elizabeth Millán-Zaibert (New York: SUNY University Press, 2004).

38 Novalis, *Fichte Studies* ed. Jane Kneller (Cambridge: Cambridge University Press, 2003), p. 185. Alison Milbank, in her newspaper article 'Gothic fiction

tells us the truth about our divided natures' (*The Guardian*, 'Comment is Free', 27 Nov. 2011), suggests that while Freud rightly saw that modernity was characterised by repression, he failed to see that it was religious consciousness itself that was repressed in the sense of the preternatural influence of the 'daemonic', that previous human cultures have mostly taken for granted.

39 Evagrius of Pontus, *The Greek Ascetic Corpus* trans. Robert E. Sinkiewicz (Oxford: Oxford University Press, 2010).

40 *FQ*, 2. *Proem*. 2–3.

41 See David Bentley Hart's fine article on Robert Kirk, 'the fairy minister': 'The Secret Commonwealth' in *First Things*, 20 October 2009.

42 See James Nohrnberg, *The Analogy of* The Faerie Queene (Princeton, NJ: Princeton University Press, 1976), pp. 762–4.

43 *FQ*, 1.10.60

44 See *FQ*, 5.7.9–11.

45 *FQ*, 1.1.40. The very last stanza of the whole poem (8.2) implies that the God of 'the host', as of the Sabbath rest, is also the God of 'the hosts' (*Sabbaoth*).

46 *FQ*, 3.6.4.

47 Envy is also the opposite of courtesy at 6.7.1.

48 See Wendy Doniger, *The Woman who Pretended to be Who She Was: Myths of Self-Imitation* (Oxford: Oxford University Press 2005) and John Milbank, *The Legend of Death: Two Poetic Sequences* (Eugene, OR: Wipf and Stock, 2008), 'Preface: the Vessel and the Ring', pp. 128–33.

49 That Una can never quite be identified as Mary, the Mother of God, is the one really shocking thing about this poem and its circumstances.

50 Purcell's semi-opera *The Fairy Queen* is in fact highly influenced by many aspects of Spenser's poem, besides Shakespeare's *Midsummer Night's Dream*.

51 I am here invoking Kierkegaard's contrast between repetition as 'recollection forwards' and recollection as 'repetition backwards'. See Soren Kierkegaard, *Fear and Trembling/Repetition,* trans. H. V. and E. H. Hong (Princeton, NJ: Princeton University Press, 1983), p. 131.

52 See *FQ*, 3. *Proem*. 1; VI. *Proem*. 4–5. Although Spenser elides medieval 'courtesy' with Renaissance 'civility', it is the sincerity of the former rather than the pragmatic formal surface peace of the latter that he clearly values. He is interested in a style of social devotion that comes from the heart and not in 'modern politeness' that is the best that permanent strangers can

come up with if they are not to kill each other. See Pickstock, *After Writing*, pp. 147–57.

53 See Regina Schwartz, *Sacramental Poetics at the Dawn of Secularism* (Stanford, CA: Stanford University Press, 2008).

54 *FQ*, 1.9.19.

55 The importance of the physical eucharist is negatively confirmed by the various figures in the book of an 'anti-eucharist' which represent a real 'physical' demonic possession: Duessa's cup of poison and the cannibalism nearly practised upon the shamefully exposed Selena: *FQ*, 1.8.14; 6.8.

56 *FQ*, 'Letter to Raleigh'. And see, for example, Wolfram von Eschenbach, *Parzival*, trans. A. T. Hatto (Harmondsworth: Penguin, 1980).

57 For example, *FQ*, 6.9.2.

58 *FQ*, 2.7.

59 See Pickstock, p. 29.

60 The Platonic dimension in *The Faerie Queene* is especially invoked in relation to the realm of Venus and her graces who dwell on Mount Acidal, since participation in the forms is primarily mediated through beauty. See *FQ*, 3.6.12.

61 *FQ*, 6.10.

62 *FQ*, 6.12.40.

63 *FQ*, 6.10.24 and footnote, p. 672. The lines here are not clear and a different arrangement may be indicated. But in any case a reciprocal spiral is clearly intended.

64 *FQ*, 7.7.7 and 41.

65 *FQ*, 7.7.59.

66 Fernando Pessoa, '*La Tempesta*/Storm' in *O Mar Sem Fim/ The Boundless Sea: Poemas de Mensagem/Poems from Mensagem* (Lisbon: Mapfre Vida, 1997).

67 *FQ*, 4.3.24; 7.7.18.

68 For this reason the juxtaposition of Spenser with Blake at the end of *Redcrosse* is wholly apposite. It is also worth mentioning that Harold Bloom thought that Spenser, after Blake, was the second great English master of the mythopoeic. See the introduction in his *Modern Critical Views: Edmund Spenser* (New York: Chelsea House, 1986), pp. 1–21.

69 *FQ*, 5. *Proem*. 3–4. This 'transvaluation of value' Spenser links to the

Renaissance myth of the return of *Astraea*, the star-exiled goddess of golden-age justice.

70 *FQ*, 3.6.47. The revolutionary transposition was first noted by C. S. Lewis. in *Studies in Medieval and Renaissance Literature* (Cambridge: Cambridge University Press, 1966), p. 155. On Burleigh and Spenser see *FQ*, IV. *Proem*.1–2 and footnote; 6.7.40–1 plus footnote, and Bruce Danner, *Edmund Spenser's War on Lord Burleigh* (London: Palgrave Macmillan, 2011). This passage in *The Faerie Queene* and many others renders implausible Richard McCabe's claim in his *Spenser's Monstrous Regiment* (Oxford: Oxford University Press, 2002) that Spenser was covertly attacking the unnatural weakness of female power. As McCabe admits, this requires one to believe that he also secretly deplores what Mikhail Bakhtin diagnosed as the 'feminine' idiom of the romance, with its repetitions, digressions and indeterminacies, over the 'masculine' linearity of the epic. In fact Spenser, in tune with his chosen genre of epic romance, oscillates between defending Grey's 'masculine' justice against Burleigh (and Elizabeth herself) and recommending her 'feminine' mercy. See further in the main text below.

71 See Nicholas P. Canny, 'Introduction: Spenser and the Reform of Ireland', in *Spenser and Ireland: An Interdisciplinary Perspective*, ed. Patricia Coughlan (Cork: Cork University Press, 1989), pp. 9–24 and 'Spenser's Irish crisis: human and experience in the 1590s', in *Past and Present* (1988), 201–9 as well as Sheila T. Cavanaugh, '"Such was Irena's Countenance": Ireland in Spenser's Poetry and Prose', in *Texas Studies in Language and Literature 2* (1986), 24–50 and '"The Fatal Destiny of that Land": Elizabethan Views of Ireland', in *Representing Ireland*, ed. Brendan Bradshaw et al. (Cambridge: Cambridge University Press, 1993), pp. 116–31. It seems fair to say that Irish (and some Irish-American) scholars tend to be less one-sidedly critical of Spenser than American ones, whose 'postcolonial' discourse is often constructed out of a complex hypocrisy about the entire matter of 'imperialism'. With far more subtlety Richard McCabe (see preceding footnote), while rightly deploring Spenser's tendency to see Gaelic culture as savage, also notes the echoed rivalry of his own and contemporary Irish Gaelic poetic projects concerning civility and even empire.

72 While he was wrong in the latter case, recent scholarship on the Celtic-Scythian relation would suggest that he was not so wildly wrong after all. See Peter S. Wells, *Beyond Celts, Germans and Scythians* (London: Duckworth), 2001.

73 See *FQ*, 4.9.40–4.

74 See *FQ*, 1.6; see also 4. *Proem*. 5 and 5.7.36–7.

75 The monarchic upholding of equity against the common law letter of precedence is an important theme in Spenser. He interestingly shared

the later Leveller delusion that the common law was something alien, introduced by the Normans. However, recent research would suggest that, indeed, post 1066 developments corrupted an original Saxon law that had more to do with the application of general principles – and so with equity – than with a slavish observation of precedent, usually established in the interests of the powerful. Here for Spenser monarchic transcendence of aristocratic height – rather like God's reach beyond the height of Jove – is, with a just condescension, on the side of the ordinary and the democratic. Spenser nonetheless thought that William the Conqueror was Edmund the Confessor's legitimate heir and that a 'strong' Norman rule had tempered the noble barbarism of the Saxons. See R. B. Seabury, 'The Norman Conquest and the Common Law: the Levellers and the Ancient Constitution' in *The Historical Journal*, 24:4 (1981), 791–806; Patrick Wormald, *The Making of English Law, Volume I* (Oxford: Blackwell, 2001).

76 Of course Conrad Noel was right to insist that Anglican Churches in England should fly the St George Cross and not the Union Jack. Yet despite being more attuned to his Christian Socialism than Andrew Shanks, I feel less attuned to his little Englandism. Even with hindsight it seems culpable beyond mere left-Woosterism to have been at once excessively condemnatory of the British empire and excessively lenient towards the Soviet one.

77 Nor of course is the United States, yet it has been and remains to a much greater degree than the UK, President Obama notwithstanding, a nation defined by 'whiteness'.

78 They were to relate, amongst much else, Arthur's conquest of Rome.

Part Two

Redcrosse

Redcrosse at St George's Chapel, Windsor. Copyright Doug Harding

Redcrosse: A New Celebration of England and St George

By Ewan Fernie, Michael Symmons Roberts, Jo Shapcott and Andrew Shanks, and featuring a new poem from Andrew Motion and the Collect for St George's Day.

N.B. What follows is the liturgical text used for the events that took place on Thursday 17 March 2011, 7.00 p.m. at St George's Chapel, Windsor and on Sunday 8 May 2011, 5.30 p.m. at Manchester Cathedral. It is hoped that it may provide the basis for other services as printed.

Redcrosse: Introductory notes

'A redcrosse knight was pricking on the plain': this is the first line of Book 1 of Edmund Spenser's epic poem *The Faerie Queene*, which is in part the inspiration of the present event. Spenser lived from c.1552 to 1599. He was not an entirely admirable man: as a colonial landowner in Ireland, his polemical contribution to Irish politics is infamous. But *The Faerie Queene* remains a great neglected masterpiece. As it exists, in unfinished form, it is divided into six large books; each with a fantastical chivalric narrative meant to illustrate a particular virtue. Book 1 has to do with 'holiness'. And the 'redcrosse knight', in his glittering armour, is eventually identified with St George.

There are various allusions to Spenser's text in what follows. The knight is a very fallible character, often led astray. At one point he is lost in a 'wandering wood'. Later, he is locked up in a giant's dungeon. When at length he comes to fight the fiery dragon, he falls into water, which magically imparts to him the strength to prevail: a symbol of God's grace.

The Fraser Chapel in Manchester Cathedral has a reredos painting by Mark Cazalet in which St George appears as a young black man in an England football shirt, amidst a scene of inner city decay. He is cutting the chains which bind a miserable looking dragon. The dragon, as always, stands for passion. But not unruly passion, needing to be subdued – rather, it is a passion for urban renewal, being liberated from despairing apathy. The 'Fire Sermon' here, written in Spenserian stanzas, alludes to this twenty-first century image; as well as to the redcrosse knight's love for his lady, Una.

We use the 400-years-old Authorized Version of the Bible ('sexist language' and all!) because of its closeness in time to Spenser, and the depth of history it evokes.

Another poet in the background is William Blake (1757–1827). Blake's text, 'And did those feet', which has become the great hymn 'Jerusalem', originally appears at the beginning of his epic *Milton*, where it is immediately followed by a line from the Bible, *Numbers* 11.29: Moses' cry, 'Would to God that all the Lord's people were Prophets!' This poetic 'Celebration of England and St George' is conceived very much in the spirit of that cry: a prayerful protest against cruder, merely propagandistic notions of patriotism. We should note that Blake was very much a rebel. The 'dark satanic mills' of his poem were, in part, intended by him as a general symbol for the Establishment. The Church of England being part of the Establishment, he would have seen this event as taking place *within* such a 'mill'. As a call to struggle against what might be called the spirit of Propaganda, 'Redcrosse' is not least a wrestling with the complex ambivalence of our history and institutions in an effort to renew and so affirm them.

In the area of Palestine, Lebanon and Syria, 'St George' is the Christian name for a figure also honoured by Muslims as 'Al Khidr', and by Jews as 'Elijah the Prophet'. Several historic figures seem to have contributed to his persona. But he has become a general symbol for the conjunction of military and political honour with religious piety. As such, he is patron saint not only of England, but also of Aragon, Catalonia, Ethiopia, Georgia, Greece, Lithuania, Montenegro, Palestine, Portugal, Russia and Serbia.

Spenser's particular contribution, however, is to make St George – in addition – a symbol of spiritual life as an unceasing, restless, troubled yet hopeful *quest* for holiness.

Redcrosse

On arrival, all members of the congregation will be given a red rose.

Introductory music

Introduction

The minister welcomes the people and then continues

Minister   Holy of Holies
All   **open our lips, our hearts, our minds**

O God, our Life, our Truth, our Way
Make us merciful, compassionate and kind

Come, God, redeem us, heal us
And grant us your peace.

Minister What is this England?
> We have a patron saint.
> What does he stand for?
> We have a flag.
> Sometimes it speaks of sporting passion. Sometimes it speaks of pomp. Sometimes it speaks of grief, at memories of war. Sometimes it speaks of vicious hatred. But when it flies upon this church it speaks of something else.
>> What is this country called to be, and to become?
>> Beyond the simple answers of the propagandists, let us dedicate ourselves today to a poetic quest.
>> Let us let ourselves be opened up. Be opened up, to one another and to God.
>> We are so many different sorts of people; let us enjoy each other's otherness.
>> And let us listen to God's elemental voice – rustling in England's green, floating in her skies, roaring in her furnaces, and rippling in her waterways.
>> Let the genius of our language lead us ever deeper, down, into the darkness of divinity.
>
> Will you join together in this quest for England and our unknown god?

All **We will.**

Musical acclamation

Reading Ephesians 6.10–18

Finally, my brethren, be strong in the Lord, and in the power of his might. Put on the whole armour of God, that ye may be able to stand against the wiles of the devil. For we wrestle not against flesh and blood, but against principalities, against powers, against the rulers of the darkness of this world, against spiritual wickedness in high places. Wherefore take unto you the whole armour of God, that ye may be able to withstand in the evil day, and having done all, to stand. Stand therefore, having your loins girt about with truth, and having on the breastplate of righteousness; And your feet shod with the preparation of the gospel of peace; Above all, taking the shield of faith, wherewith ye shall be able to quench all the fiery darts of the wicked. And take the helmet of salvation, and the sword of the Spirit, which is the word of God: Praying always with all prayer and supplication in the Spirit, and watching thereunto with all perseverance and supplication for all saints.

> Minister I now humbly charge *you*, also, to don that armour. Let it shine with your resolve to seek, to serve; to serve by seeking. Faith in the unknown God is hard, but, beyond all winning and having, it is outpoured love.
>
> And here we have our surrogate and champion in the consequent adventure. Here is *St George*: a George whose destiny it is to be forever young and full of dreams; forever changed and changing in the quest; much like ourselves in his confusion and his straying; a troubled soul, in search of truth: the symbol of our restlessness.
>
> Will you accept him as your representative?
>
> All **Yes, indeed we will.**

St George music

Redcrosse   Andrew Motion

> When it was time for the field full of folk to go dark,
> and the folk themselves to be splintered in clans

then wander away to their homes and their trades,

one particular fellow, a pilgrim, swerved off alone.
He holds our attention. He might even be reckoned
to beckon us over his shoulder to follow his story.

We cannot resist. Why would we? The way we exist
depends on him. But that reminds me. Is he a man
or a woman? And is this a sudden decision or some-

thing he kept up his sleeve? There is no way of telling,
except that I see he has taken to losing himself in the forest
one minute, and making his living there robbing the rich,

and the next has abandoned all this for a spell in the city
where hammers have beaten his kindness into new shapes.
These he accepts, although you might call them the duty

of state. Which reminds me. What is he called? Forget that.
The greatest mystery facing us now is how to keep faith
as we follow him over the latest threshold, into the world

where everything flashes its label, and we expect to be
getting the dirt, or at least the drift. Let me say it again.
How to keep faith. Here in the field where the grass

has recovered but we have forgotten its names,
and clouds that are carved in the shape of a cave
pour forth in torrents of melting silver the rain.

Silence is kept

    Minister   'A redcrosse knight was pricking on the plain'
    All   **Let us follow where he wanders.**

St George music

    All   **Desire, death-marked and questing, though in vain,**
                      still questing, always questing,
                            and in that questing free,
                      still yearning, only yearning, for by that yearning we
                      may find that life beyond life,
                          which is what it means to be.

    Minister   O God of infinite harmony, we are but fragments;
                      knit us into a rich and teeming wholeness!

The Four Stations of the Elements

    Minister   And now we are armed and ready to go together as
                      if to encounter life for the first time. Our scene is a
                      wandering wood –

Wandering Wood music

What the Forest Said   Jo Shapcott

You think we don't know you are there,
but the sun glints you so brightly
among the far leaves, we feel your heat

from miles away. You just shine
with your reflective face, your human light.
When you arrive, forget how to smell pine sap, don't

notice the pattern of cones on the path
as you pass, or the snap of twigs. Don't touch the cedar's bark
to feel its distinctive gnarl, nor stroke the viney elm.

Just head for the bower at the heart, don't think
cave, or error, past or present. By now
you'll want to be lost, so don't glance back

down the trails to notice how different it all
looks in reverse: how the aspen, the oak
and the poplar turn, in a twist, to poplar, oak, aspen.

Have the trees moved? Or is it you?
Go off course in time, too, so's not to
remember how long it took to hike

from the dark cypress to the bent laurel,
then past the tall fir next to the weeping willow.
Every route's a story and a teller finds

the way by stitching trees together in a tale: how
the yew bent down to stroke the earth and everything
under it, how birch shafts held up the sky.

Don't get lost in stories, if you want to get lost in a wood
and, at this juncture, you really do – with that look
of embowerment softening your eyes.

Don't stop moving, don't pitch up under the sallow,
or drop and wait for rescue under the unlikely myrrh.
Keep wandering, noting how the paths bend together

and sway apart in a rhythm which owes everything
to beech and ash in the wind, to green leaves blocking the sun.
Where do you think you are

as you pass olive trees and plantains
and holm oaks in the dusk, hoping
for a kind grove ahead, a bower

of familiar maples, not this branching
trail which expands and contracts around you,
a green cave in which you know you will go so wrong.

Silence is kept

Minister   Come, God as yet unknown. As we, like George, go travelling in the Spirit, lead us through confusion. And purge us from our past mistakes.

We pray:

All   **O God, we have gone wrong,**
and wandered like lost sheep.
We heard your call,
it touched our hearts,
but surface things seduced us.
Spoilt, then, we present ourselves
before your face, and beg to be forgiven.

Minister   Now come with me, further, into the labyrinth –

Air music

Air: A Psalm of Many Voices   Andrew Shanks

1

Listen to the silent trouble in the air:
the hidden hubbub of your neighbours' babbled prayers.

'Lord!' 'Hallelujah! (Halle-lujah?)' 'Hear!' 'Have mercy!' 'Help!'
'O, Come!' 'Save!' 'Heal!' 'And grant us peace!'

In the leaves, a rustling restlessness:
'Where now? There's no clear path. I've gone astray!'

And murmuring, beneath the proud world's steamy din:
'Why? *Why* do I do this? I've no idea!'

Or, in the stillness of the giant's pit:
'Here – craving your forgiveness – I despair.'

Until, at length, somewhere a key creaks in a lock:
and then – fresh oxygen (thank God) floods in.

'Breathe freely now!
The "God" you thought you knew – that *wasn't* God.'

2

Sunlight, as it dances on the knight's hacked helm,
   picks out old marks of battle, asking:
'What caused these?'

Air reaches for the flag he holds; folds, flips and fingers it,
   caressingly:
'What hopes are meant by this?'

Whatever is of heaven flares and flutters:
Nothing is simple, nothing's ever fixed.

His banner, then – it joins two colours:
two prime elements.

One's the effulgence of the sacramental word:
'Let there be light!' till kingdom come, when all at last is lit.

The other, daubed across, is:
Abel's rose-red blood.

So Air unfolds it, flaps it out:
'The "God" you thought you knew – that wasn't God.'

'But here's the standard of the One:
you ought to know you do not know.'

For, 'Everything's double':
cry the canny Clouds, on high.

'Cain, *also*, is a shepherd
herding human sheep.'

'Whatever is of heaven flares and flutters:
Nothing is simple, nothing's ever fixed.'

Silence is kept

    Minister   May the universal God, our heavenly Encourager,
                    who urges us to find within our quest
                    the joy of perfect freedom,
                    pardon all you who truly repent:
                    wash you clean of your sin;
                    make you strong as sturdy wood;
                    touch your hearts with fire;
                    revive you with the oxygen of honesty.
                    May your chastened life make manifest
                    the openness that will unite us all at last.
                    In Jesus' name. Amen

    Minister   And now – brace yourselves
                    to go, together, into the dragon's mouth!

Fire music

The Fire Sermon   Ewan Fernie

    I am the voice of fire, I am the dragon's breath!
        I'm a voice so hot it burns like an angry sun!

Hot air wafts pride, but fire cremates death,
Until all flesh that flowers and rots is gone
And what remains is spirit all alone
To throw itself in any glowing form
New life presents and quest will make undone,
Reshaping as its own what still is warm!
Oh, every questing George should love his fire-breathing worm!

You were a George in red – a black George –
   You'd come down the river during your break, to think
   And be alone, away from the hot forge
   Of the kitchen, and found a gang, starting to drink,
   A mixed group, ten or twelve. One girl winked:
   You were rooted and mated, your desires mirrored!
   But what swept you onward to a further brink
   Was her special kind of stillness – stillness that *shimmered*
And pricked and lit your tears while they tumbled forth and glimmered.

And comforting and lovely blandishment
   She tendered, charging you always to hold her dear,
   For sure, she swore, her love was on you bent
   From now till Judgement Day, so you should never fear.
   And whether this was true or to stem your tears,
   No human heart was ever more ravished with delight,
   No living ear before or since more soothing words did hear,
   As her lips murmured to you that far-off, heaven-sent night
Before their parting whisper, 'Now for me you must *fight*.'

But when you woke and found that she was gone,
   And nothing but pressed grass where you had lain,
   You stormed and raged to lose all you'd won,

Watering her place with tears throughout the day.
But from that time your element is flame,
And all your days you've loved her face divine,
And tirelessly fought and forged desire's burning way
Vowing never to rest until at last you find
She for whom you search, in fantasising mind.

My way of flame has touched your heart and face
With love, divorce and infidelity,
With this girl's glance, and with that boy's grace,
With glamour, power and celebrity.
At times from dragons you may turn and flee,
But you have learned when you my kin must slay
And you know now when you must set us free
And when to soothe and stroke and make us tame
And when to mount and ride and set the heavens aflame!

When one day, dragon-borne, you drop from the sky,
Diminishing like a golden pea,
Charting the course of your own last sigh
That quickly nothing is but vacancy,
Then will you perceive life's agony
As lineaments of her face divine,
And struggle will seem an ecstasy,
Failure a thronging diamond mine,
The gift of this knowledge, the gift of the courage to die.

Silence is kept

Minister	O God, when we are helpless, lost, alone
All	**Guide us**

When we are speechless in the face of evil and injustice

Inspire us

When we turn away from you towards false gods
Rescue us

When we fear that we have lost the fight
Renew our strength

Let us join together in the Lord's Prayer:

All   **Our Father, who art in heaven,**
hallowed be thy name;
thy kingdom come;
thy will be done,
in earth as it is in heaven.
Give us this day our daily bread.
And forgive us our trespasses,
as we forgive them that trespass against us.
And lead us not into temptation;
but deliver us from evil.
For thine is the kingdom,
the power, and the glory,
for ever and ever.
Amen.

Minister   And follow me, now, to where freshness springs –

Water music

Water Song   Michael Symmons Roberts

I can drown you, slake you or baptise,
can hold you, but cannot be held for long,
am in you as the fall is in the rise.

How do I begin? With rain's dash on stone,
with cool flight of zephyr off the sea
that scales a mountain's face, then

lets *me* loose; a mist, a spit, a flurry,
down to earth, through fissures, gathering
my powers in the dark, to carry

silver out in a rush you call a spring.
Wash your face. In my light-folds, otters
twist for eels, kingfishers catch mayflies. *Drink.*

Here you wrestle angels. Water. *Utter.*
What can a wounded warrior do,
but let my wound-salve rinse him better?

So it was that George, the one who
felled the beast, fell into me; bruised and beaten.
Day one: dragon rose, near-slew

my man, and tipped him in to drown.
Hold him. I healed him in my silent
heart and kept him down until the burn,

the multi-angled careless sun, was spent.
Then up he gasped, remade. For *spring*,
read *source*. I make so many rivers I lose count.

A stream can be crossed with a single
step, but I have mighty mouths, where
Thames and Severn, Tyne and Avon, England's

waters break as island dry land tapers,
where fresh gives way to salt,
in currents stitched with weed and elvers.

Does water have a memory? Did his cuts
give me this crimson tint?
It was George who split the dragon's throat,

who fought until his sword was blunt.
But beast fell ghost, and George fell to his knees.
He gazed along the line of my descent:

from spring to pool, from tributary
to river, estuary to shallows,
out towards the glorious, the terrifying sea.

Silence is kept

Minister	Sisters and brothers, we have come together to seek for God in the basic elements and scenes of living: in the mazy shade of *woods*; in the volatile embrace of *air*; in the blazing rage of *flame*; and in sheer liquid *water*.
	Everywhere: the throb of *blood*. Of our own lifeblood, not earned but given us; and of God's blood; the red of that Red Cross which is the symbol, flag and banner of our nation.
All	**Wood, and air, and fire, and water drawn together and quartered by blood, in sign of our common life, prayer, and our creative strife:**
	O, may we be one in the struggle.

Musical acclamation

Sacramental making of the Red Cross

Readers and actors assemble the new red cross during an extended musical interlude.

Collect of St George

Minister God of hosts,
who so kindled the flame of love
in the heart of your servant George
that he bore witness to the risen Lord
by his life and by his death:
give us the same faith and power of love
that we who rejoice in his triumphs
may come to share with him
the fullness of the resurrection;
through Jesus Christ your Son our Lord,
who is alive and reigns with you,
in the unity of the Holy Spirit,
one God, now and for ever.
Amen.

Musical acclamation

Hymn

And did those feet in ancient time.
Walk upon England's mountains green:
And was the holy Lamb of God,
On England's pleasant pastures seen!

And did the Countenance Divine,
Shine forth upon our clouded hills?
And was Jerusalem builded here,
Among these dark Satanic Mills?

Bring me my Bow of burning gold;
Bring me my Arrows of desire:
Bring me my Spear: O clouds unfold!
Bring me my Chariot of fire!

I will not cease from Mental Fight,
Nor shall my Sword sleep in my hand:
Till we have built Jerusalem,
In England's green and pleasant Land

C. Hubert H. Parry   William Blake

Blessing

Minister   Would to God that all the Lord's people were prophets!
          God bless you. Amen.

The red cross is raised and the Choir departs, singing.

*The red cross made of roses, Redcrosse at St George's Chapel, Windsor.
Copyright Doug Harding*

Index

Abel 86
Alberge, Dalya 35
allegory 18–19, 23, 51–3, 106, 109,
    125–6, 137, 140–2, 145–6,
    149–62
  Christian 151, 153, 159
  pagan 151, 153
  poetic 141–2, 151, 159
  realism of 154, 160
  theological 141–2
Amos (Hebrew prophet) 65
Anglicanism 13, 15, 27, 30–1, 34, 73,
    121–3, 133–4, 182
Apetrei, Sarah xiii, 18, 25, 28, 33
Apuleius 153

Badiou, Alain 149
Battle of the Flags 79–83
Behring Breivik, Anders 31
Bellah, Robert 60–1
Benedict XVI, Pope 98
Benjamin, Walter 151
Bennett, Gareth 121
Berryman, John 97–9
The Birmingham Post 33
Blake, William 65, 75, 97, 152, 182,
    198
Book of Common Prayer (BCP)
    27–31, 120–1

Booth Centre for the Homeless 8,
    71, 76
Botticelli, Sandro 164
British National Party (BNP) 6,
    13–14, 54, 68–78, 96
Brooke, Rupert 95
Bunyan, John 25, 152–3
Burleigh, Lord 168

Cain and the Cain-principle 86
Campaign for Nuclear Disarmament
    60
Catholicism 94, 98, 136, 160–1
Cazalet, Mark 28, 34, 38, 69–70, 182
charismatic movement 106–7
Christian Socialism 83
Church of England *see* Anglicanism
Coleridge, Samuel Taylor 152
common prayer, rite of 27–31, 36
    see also Book of Common
    Prayer
Conrad, Joseph 47
corruption in contemporary life 116
Coventry Cathedral 7, 41
Cranmer, Thomas 27, 30, 119–21
critical creative culture 10–12

Daily Mail 72, 134–5
Daily Star 35

Index

Dante Alighieri 48–9, 140–3, 146–9
de Man, Paul 151–3
Devereaux, Paul 8, 71
Dickinson, Emily 97
Donne, John 97, 161
dragon-slaying myths 111–13, 122, 129, 136, 160, 182
Drayton, Michael 143
dreams 50

Elizabeth the First 15, 138, 162, 170–1
Englishness 4–5, 9, 12–14, 26, 36, 38, 60, 79, 95–9, 133–5, 166
Eusebius 110
Evagrius Pontus 155
Evening Prayer, order of 28–9, 60, 150

The Faerie Queene 16–26, 37, 45–6, 51–3, 84–5, 95–9, 106, 108, 124–6, 134–49, 155–6, 159–67, 181
fairy tales 46, 49–50, 53
fascism 81–3
Fernie, Ewan xiii–xiv, 66, 69, 96, 105, 113, 124, 139, 147, 191
'The Fire Sermon' (poem) 38–9, 139, 191–3
Freedom News Network 75
Freud, Sigmund 154–5

Garland, Tim 8, 40, 140
gender issues 32–3, 107–9
Grasmere 125–6
Greenblatt, Stephen 9–10
Grey, Lord 168
Griffin, Nick 7
The Guardian 35

Hamann, J. G. 152
Hegel, G. W. F. 85–8

heroic attitude 53–4
Hölderlin, Friedrich 65
Holderness, Graham 32
Holst, Gustav 79
Homer 51–2, 153
Hugo, Victor 154
Hume, David 149
Hungary 135
Hussain, Monawar 113
Hutchinson, Mary 126

iconoclasm 122
The Independent 73
individualism and individuation 112
Ireland 168–71, 181

Jennings, Elizabeth 18
'Jerusalem' (hymn) 41, 75, 182, 197–8
Jesus Christ 32–3, 40, 49–51, 58–9, 65, 97–8, 113, 150, 153
Jones, David 99–100
Jonson, Ben 16
Jung, Carl Gustav (and Jungian analysis) 111–13, 119, 128, 155

Kanuik, Ross 72
Kipling, Rudyard 95, 135

Law, William 123
literary scholarship and criticism 9–10, 95
liturgy 50, 53–4, 67, 83–4, 88, 93–8, 119–22, 151, 166
  versus propaganda 57–66, 84–5, 147–8
  see also *Redrosse* liturgy
Lloyd, Vincent 62–3
The Lord's Prayer 150, 194
Luther, Martin (and Lutheranism) 65, 122

Index

Man Booker prize 46
Manchester Cathedral 68–9, 71, 96, 101
   reredos painting 6–7, 28, 34–6, 70–1, 182
Manchester Evening News 82
Marvell, Andrew 49
Marx, Karl 15
Mass, the 94
metaphor 151–2, 159
Milbank, John xiv, 24–5
Miles Platting 76
Milton, John 155, 161
Moore, Robert 123
Motion, Andrew xiv, 6, 8, 33, 37, 96, 116, 119, 138, 185
multiculturalism 30, 34
Murray, Les 30
myths 48, 50 *see also* dragon-slaying myths

National Front 7, 36
nationalism 14, 54, 95, 108, 112
naturalism 46–7, 50
Neoplatonism 155
Noel, Conrad 79–83
norms 62–3
Novalis 154–5

Odysseus and *The Odyssey* 48, 51–2
Origen 142, 153
'original sin', concept of 67–8, 117
Owen, Wilfred 95

panpsychism 155
Pargeter, Edith 124
Parry, Hubert 198
participation 9–11
'pathos', religious 64–5
patriotism 12–15, 32, 35, 68, 114–15, 129, 135

Pessoa, Fernando 167
Pickstock, Catherine 62–3, 93, 150
Platonism 166 *see also* Neoplatonism
postcolonial criticism 14
Prayer Book Society 34
propaganda 57–9, 63–5, 68, 83
'A Psalm of Many Voices' 37–8, 84, 86, 127, 139, 189–91
Pseudo-Dionysius 85

radio commissions 97
Read, Sam 125
realism and reality 47–50, 155–7, 160
'red', double meaning of 144–6
red cross symbol 31, 36, 95, 100–1, 114, 118, 145
red rose symbol 40, 86–7, 101, 139, 199
'Redcrosse' (poem) 6, 37, 119, 137–8, 185–6
Redcrosse knight (in *The Faerie Queene*) 23–8, 49, 51, 53, 66, 78, 84–6, 99–100, 106–13, 124–8, 136–9, 143–4, 157, 160, 182
Redcrosse liturgy 3, 7–18, 24, 27–8, 31, 34–41, 61–8, 74, 76, 84, 95, 98–101, 105–12, 119, 133, 139–40, 145, 147, 150–1, 159–62, 167, 170
religion 13–15, 26, 109
   civil 36, 60, 166
Rosicrucianism 87–8
Royal Holloway College Choir xv, 8
Royal Shakespeare Company (RSC) 7–8, 41
Ruskin, John 137, 169–70

Sachs, Nelly 65
St George 9, 12–14, 24–8, 31–3, 38–40, 60, 64, 68–9, 95, 109,

111, 115, 127, 136, 150, 156,
    161, 171, 182–3
ambiguities of 77–83
cult of 135
portrayed as a black youth 2, 6–7,
    34–8, 41, 69, 72, 182
shrine of 79
tomb of 78
St George and the Dragon, giant
    figures of 6–7, 70–2, 76, 78
St George's Chapel, Windsor 4–5, 96,
    101, 178, 199
St George's Day 4, 7, 11, 14, 24, 36,
    68–9, 72–3, 76, 95–6, 101, 148
    collect for 129, 197
St George's House, Windsor 118–19
St Patrick 136
St Paul 20, 33, 54, 106, 109, 150, 155
Sassoon, Siegfried 95
Schlegel, Friedrich 151–2
sermons as a literary form 93
'shakenness' (Shanks) 62, 65–8, 146
Shakespeare, William 52, 154, 161
Shanks, Andrew xiv–xv, 3, 8, 27, 31,
    34, 37, 54, 56, 73–5, 96, 127,
    137, 139, 146–51, 189
Shapcott, Jo xv, 8, 37, 96, 162–3, 187
Singleton, Charles 142
slander 167–70
Spenser, Edmund 4, 8–10, 15–28,
    33, 37–40, 45–6, 51–3, 66,
    78, 84–5, 99, 106, 108–10,
    119, 125, 135–40, 143–71,
    181, 183
spiritual warfare 110, 113, 124, 156
spirituality 100, 109, 151
Stevens, Wallace 47–8
Sutherland, Graham 41
Symmons Roberts, Michael xv, 8, 39,
    76, 113, 160, 194

The Tablet 97
Taylor, Andrew 31
Thaxted 79–83
Thomas, Edward 100
Traherne, Thomas 161

Vernunft and *Verstand* 87–9
Vickers, Salley xv–xvi, 18, 111
Vico, Giambattista 169

Warwick, Daisy, Countess of 79
'Water Song' (poem) 39, 13–14, 160,
    194–6
Waterstone's (booksellers) 46
'What the Forest Said' (poem) 38,
    162, 187–9
Williams, Rowan 114–15, 117, 120
Windsor Spring Festival 4
witchcraft and witch-hunting 107–9
Woodman, Marion 112–13
Wordsworth, William 9, 125–6